JAMES W. MOORE

GOD WAS HERE, & I WAS OUT TO LUNCH

DIMENSIONS
FOR LIVING
NASHVILLE

GOD WAS HERE, AND I WAS OUT TO LUNCH

This book is printed on acid-free paper.

Library of Congress Cataloging-in-Publication Data

Moore, James W. (James Wendell), 1938-
God was here and I was out to lunch / James W. Moore.
 p. cm.
ISBN 0-687-09722-3 (alk. paper)
 1. Christian life—Methodist authors.   1. Title.
BV4501.3 .M66 2001
248.4—dc21

                                                                2001042235

02 03 04 05 06 07 08 09 10 — 10 9 8 7 6 5 4

MANUFACTURED IN THE UNITED STATES OF AMERICA

For
Ashley,
Brantley, Tonya, Macey Rae,
Cissy, Ed, Jim, Christian,
Jeff, Claire, Dawson, Baby Moore,
Jodi, Danny, Sarah, Paul,
Julie,
Leslie, Ric,
Wendell, Bettina, Caroline, Kelsey, Preston

Contents

Introduction

God Was Here, and
I Was Out to Lunch

Scripture: Mark 3:1-6; Genesis 28:16

Way back in the book of Genesis, Jacob made a powerful and poignant statement that has resounded across the ages. He said, "Surely the LORD is in this place—and I did not know it!" The modern-day version of that statement would sound something like this: "God was here, and I was out to lunch!" Both of these statements underscore an oft-repeated happening in life, namely this: God comes near us, and we are so busy, so preoccupied, so set in our ways, or so caught up in our own agenda that we don't recognize God; we don't sense God's presence. Let me show you what I mean.

A seasoned senior angel was giving a brand-new freshman angel a tour of the heavens. The freshman angel was wide-eyed and awestruck as he saw the vastness and majesty and wonder of God's incredible universe. When they came to the Milky Way, the mature senior angel said to the freshman angel, "Come over here, son, I want to show you something special. Look down there! That tiny planet is called Earth. It looks rather insignificant from here, doesn't it? It looks so small and so inconsequential, but something quite remarkable happened there some years ago. You see, the people of Earth had gotten off the track a bit. They were missing the whole point of their existence. They were missing the meaning of life. So God sent his only Son into that world to save

7

the people and to teach them what God meant life to be for them on Earth."

"Wow! That's amazing!" said the freshman angel excitedly. "You mean to tell me that God's Son actually visited that little planet? How pleased the people of Earth must have been to receive him! I can just imagine that they must have had a great celebration for him on Earth."

"No," said the senior angel quietly. Then, with tears glistening in his eyes, he said, "No—they tried to kill him! They were so wrapped up in their old, rigid ways of doing things that when God's Son presented some new ideas, they resented him, and they tried to silence him. Blinded by the old, they missed the new. Surely the Lord was in that place, and they did not know it. God was there, and they were out to lunch!"

How easy it is to fall into this trap! How easy it is to become so paralyzed by our usual ways of doing things that new ways threaten the life out of us! How easy it is to become so closed minded that we are blind to any kind of new truth! Blinded by the forms, we miss the force! Blinded by our rituals, we miss our reason for being! Blinded by our narrowness, we miss God's nearness. Blinded by the old, we miss the new!

We see a vivid example of this in the third chapter of the Gospel of Mark. As early as Mark 3, Jesus is already a "marked man." As early as Mark 3, powerful religious leaders of the day were out to get him. The Pharisees, the Sadducees, and the priests—all were so threatened by Jesus that they had been watching him, looking for a way to trap him, to trip him up and to do him in. Jesus went into the synagogue on the Sabbath; it was his custom to worship there on this holy day, and he would not be "frightened off" by nervous but powerful authority figures.

They were there! In the synagogue that day there was a "watchdog" group, a deputation team from the Sanhedrin. These persons saw Jesus as a troublemaker, and they were there to keep an eye on him. No one could miss them, because in the synagogue the front seats were the seats of honor, and these leaders were sitting there. It was the duty of this group to deal with anyone who was likely to mislead the people. So they were there that day not to worship or to learn. They were there to scrutinize Jesus, to watch critically his every action, and to listen cautiously and cynically to his every word.

Now, also in the synagogue that day, there was a man with a withered hand. His hand was paralyzed. The Greek word used to describe the condition of his hand suggests that he had not been born that way, but rather some illness or injury had taken the strength from him. Other writings (notably the Gospel according to the Hebrews, which is a Gospel lost except for a few fragments) tell us that the man was a stonemason and that he had come to Jesus for help because his livelihood was in the use of his hands, and he didn't want to beg for food or money.

Now, if Jesus had been a frightened man, he would have looked the other way or perhaps arranged to meet with this man the next day, because he knew that he was being watched, and he knew that if he helped this man he would be asking for trouble—BIG trouble! Because this was the Sabbath day, all forms of work were forbidden, and to heal a person was considered work. What to do? The people present wondered and murmured. The Pharisees watched intently. This was the test. "What is Jesus going to do now? Will he heal this man on the Sabbath? If he does, he will be in trouble with the Law." As often was the case with Jesus, the real question was, Which is the more important thing—the law or the human being?

9

Jesus turned to those gathered around and asked, "What is the right thing to do—to take life or to save life?" Don't miss the subtle point here. Jesus knew that the Pharisees were plotting against his life, and so he had asked, "Is it right to take life or to save life?" The onlookers said nothing. Then Jesus said to the man with the withered hand, "Stretch forth your hand!" The man did as Jesus said, and he was healed.

Think about the implications: The man was healed. He was made well. He could go back to his job now. He could shake hands now. He could be considered a full member of the day's society again. He could have new life! Well, what do you think happened next; was there great rejoicing in the synagogue? Did they all live happily ever after? Was this the end of the story? No! Not quite! Listen to the last sentence: "The Pharisees went out and immediately conspired with the Herodians against [Jesus], how to destroy him" (Mark 3:6).

Jesus had done a great thing, and yet they did not rejoice. Instead, they sought to destroy him, and—don't miss this, now—they "conspired with the Herodians." Who were the Herodians? They were the court entourage of King Herod. This shows how scared and desperate the Pharisees really were. Normally, they wouldn't have had anything to do with the Herodians. Normally, they considered the Herodians unclean. But now, they were so resentful of Jesus, so jealous, that they were prepared to enter into what was for them an unholy alliance.

The Pharisees plotted with the Herodians against Jesus to destroy him. That's how the story ends. Blinded by their hostility, they missed the holiness. Blinded by their hatred, they missed the healing. Blinded by their duty, they missed the divinity. Blinded by the old way, they missed the new way. To the Pharisee, religion was ritual; religion meant obeying certain rules and regulations. If you kept the rules, you were good. If you broke the rules, you were bad. Jesus broke these regulations, and the Pharisees were genuinely convinced that he was a troublemaker and needed to be silenced for the good of the community.

On the other hand, to Jesus religion meant service, caring, loving, helping, healing. It meant love of God and love of people. Ritual was irrelevant unless it produced love in action. Jesus spoke strong words about this in Matthew's Gospel:

> "Woe to you, scribes and Pharisees, hypocrites! For you tithe mint, dill, and cummin, and have neglected the weightier matters of the law: justice and mercy and faith. It is these you ought to have practiced without neglecting the others. You blind guides! You strain out a gnat but swallow a camel!" (Matthew 23:23-34)

To Jesus, the most important thing in the world was not the correct performance of a ritual, but the spontaneous, compassionate answer to the cry of human need. But we have to admit it. We must confess that often, even today, like the Pharisees, we are so blinded by the old that we miss the new. God comes near, but we are out to lunch. Let me be more specific.

Sometimes, Blinded by the Law, We Miss the Chance to Love

Blinded by law, we miss the love! That's what happened to the Pharisees that day. They were so alarmed and so upset when they saw Jesus break the Sabbath law that they were completely blinded to the compassionate and wonderfully loving thing that he had done! He had helped a man, healed a man, changed his life, and they didn't even see it. They were blinded by their rules. They were blinded by their laws. Blinded by the law, they missed the love! "Surely the Lord was in that place—and they did not know it." Let me bring this closer to home with a true story.

It happened in a Southern city just a few years ago. Steve and his wife, Trudy, were building a new home on the lake. Late one afternoon as they were inspecting the progress on their new house, they heard their daughter's screams from the water's edge, where she had been playing. Their daughter Allison had been bitten by a three-foot-long copperhead snake! There was no phone, so there was no way to call an ambulance. So Steve and Trudy did what you and I probably would have done. Time was of the essence, so they scooped Alison up into loving arms, jumped into their car, and made a mad dash to the nearest hospital. With the car's emergency flasher-lights on and the horn blasting, they drove frantically through the streets in search of medical help for their daughter. It was a horrifying, life-or-death situation. Finally, they arrived at a hospital and rushed into the emergency room, where a talented team of doctors and nurses worked with care and precision (over the next seven days) to save Allison's life.

But when her father came out of the emergency room, he was met by a police officer who ticketed him for five traffic violations—speeding, running a red light, running a stop sign, reckless driving, and disturbing the peace—and he was put on probation.

This story shows vividly the weakness of legalism. Now, please don't misunderstand me. I'm not fussing at the law. I know that we have to have laws. I'm not criticizing that police officer. He was simply doing his duty as he saw it. I am simply saying that there are times when human need must transcend the law. There are times when love and understanding and compassion must supersede the law. I'm glad that Jesus was a child of grace and a servant of love rather than a slave of law. Sometimes, blinded by the law, we miss the love.

Sometimes, Blinded by Common Practice, We Miss the Common Sense

The Pharisees were so trapped in their usual, rigid, common ways of doing things that they were blind to the common sense of helping a man in need. Do you recall the classic story about the young man who found his new wife in the kitchen preparing a roast for dinner? Very carefully, she cut the roast in half. Then, very conscientiously, she put half in one pan and the other half in another pan and then put them in the oven. Puzzled, her husband asked her why she had cut the roast in half and put the halves in separate pans. "I've always done it that way," she answered.

"But why?" persisted the husband.

"Well, because *Mom* did it that way."

The husband picked up the phone and called his wife's mother, and he asked her why she had always cut the roast in half and baked the halves in two separate pans. His mother-in-law replied, "Because *Grandma* did it that way."

When the couple asked Grandma why she too had followed this practice, her explanation was simple: She had never owned a pan big enough to hold an entire roast!

Now, this is a light illustration of a very significant point, namely, that we can get so locked into certain ways of doing things that we fail to consider whether they are right or wrong or whether they make sense.

That's what happened to the Pharisees. They had gotten so accustomed to doing things a certain way, that they were not open to any new way, even though it made sense. They couldn't understand the common sense of Jesus in helping this man because their common practice was to not help people on the Sabbath.

Blinded by the law, we can miss the chance to love. Blinded by common practice, we miss the common sense.

And Finally, Blinded by Our Systems, We Miss the Savior

We see it graphically in Mark 3. The Son of God walked into the Pharisees' lives, and they tried to kill him. He tried to teach them love, and they would not listen. They had their ways, they had their systems, and Jesus was upsetting their apple cart, so they plotted against him. God was here, and they were out to lunch!

One Sunday morning a number of years ago, during Sunday school in the church I was serving, a ninth grader turned on the fire alarm. Bells began ringing loudly, and in just a few moments three fire trucks with sirens blaring were there to answer the false alarm. When we asked the ninth grader why he had turned on the fire alarm, he said, "I didn't think it would work!"

Isn't that what we say to God? On page after page of the Scriptures, God urges us to put love first, to have goodwill toward all people, to pray for others, to help others, to care for others, to serve others. Supremely in Jesus, God shows us that love is the answer, love is the way, love is what God wants; but we don't think it will work. We rely on power plays and hostile threats and political strategies and bureaucratic systems. We plot against one another. We flog one another with cruel words and deadly gossip. We crucify one another trying to get our way. We don't quite trust love yet. We don't think it will work.

14

Well, let me tell you something: God showed us it works—on a cross! There at the cross, God showed us that love—not laws, not practices, not systems, but *love*—is the most powerful thing in the world!

Will you try it? Will you try it completely for one day? If you would live totally in the Spirit of love for one day, it would change your life forever!

❧ 1 ❧

Don't Miss . . .
The Call to Discipleship

Scripture: Mark 1:16-20

*T*his is a true story, but one that may make you say, "Only in California." Larry Walters was a thirty-something truck driver who lived in Los Angeles. He lived in one of those neighborhoods where all of the houses looked alike, and where each of the yards was surrounded by a chain-link fence. Every Saturday afternoon, Larry had a ritual. He would sit in a lawn chair, sip a cool beverage, and just relax for a couple of hours. This is what he would do every Saturday afternoon in his backyard.

One Saturday, however, Larry got a bright idea. He decided that he would tie some helium balloons to his lawn chair, enough to float himself about one hundred feet or so over his neighbors' yards. It should be noted at this point that Larry was not an aeronautics engineer. Therefore, he didn't *really* know how many helium balloons it would take to elevate him to the desired height of one hundred feet.

So Larry purchased forty-five weather balloons and filled them with helium. Then he packed some sandwiches, prepared his cool beverage, and took along a BB gun so that he could shoot out one or more of the balloons if he got too high. Next, with the help of his neighbors, he tied the balloons to his lawn chair. (Let me digress just long enough to say: "Don't try this at home!")

At the appropriate signal, the neighbors let go of the ropes that tethered the "balloon-chair." Larry immediately rocketed up to 11,000 feet! No kidding! He was so shocked and so frightened, that he never got a chance to shoot any of the balloons out with his BB gun; instead, he was too busy holding on to the lawn chair.

Larry was first spotted by a DC-10 pilot flying into Los Angeles International Airport; he had zipped up into one of the busiest flight patterns in the world. The DC-10 pilot radioed the tower that there was a man on a lawn chair at 11,000 feet, and that he had a gun! Planes were immediately rerouted around the spot where Larry was floating. Rescue craft were sent up, and eventually they got Larry safely back down to the ground with his lawn chair. He was, of course, quickly surrounded by reporters who had rushed out to get the story on this bizarre (even for California) event. Reporters asked Larry, "Were you scared?"

"No," Larry said.

"Would you do it again?"

"No."

"Well, why did you do it in the first place?"

Larry replied, "Well—you can't just *sit* there!"

Now, strange as it may seem, when I first heard the story of Larry's big adventure that Saturday afternoon in Los Angeles, it made me think of the first chapter of Mark, where Jesus came to Simon, Andrew, James, and John at the seashore and called them to be his disciples. In effect, Jesus said to them: Don't just sit there doing the same old things, performing the same old rituals, living the same old life. Break out of the drudgery! Do something good—exciting—come and follow me!

Please don't misunderstand me. I am not applauding Larry and his lawn chair and helium balloons. Obviously, that was a dangerous and crazy thing to do. He could have been killed. He could have caused all kinds of problems, and in fact, he did. He could have hurt someone else. Indeed, his exploits that day could have produced a major calamity. But even though he went about it the wrong way, what is significant to notice here is this: There was something stirring deep down inside of Larry, telling him that just sitting there was not enough. There is more to life than just sitting there.

This is precisely the way Simon, Andrew, James, and John must have been feeling that day when Jesus walked into their lives. They were suffering under Roman oppression, with Roman soldiers swaggering about, barking commands that must be obeyed "or else." They were working hard as fishermen, but much of the fruit of their labor was going to pay Roman taxes. And on top of that, the Temple authorities were giving them a rough time and demanding more and more of their resources. Life was a difficult grind for them. They were "going through the motions," but they felt defeated and apathetic and hopeless. They felt bored and trapped in this vicious cycle and could see no way out. Let me ask you something. Have you ever felt that way? Do you feel that way right now?

A businessman checked into a hotel late one night. He decided that he would stop in the lounge for a few minutes before going up to his room. Later that night, he called the front desk and asked, "What time will the lounge be opened in the morning?" The night clerk answered, "9:00 A.M." About an hour later, the man called again with the same question: "What time will the lounge be opened in the morning?" Again the clerk said, "9:00 A.M." The man called a third time, and a fourth, and every hour throughout the night. Each time the night clerk would answer: "9:00 A.M."

At 7:00 A.M. the hotel manager arrived, and the night

clerk reported that everything had gone all right, except
for this crazy man who kept calling the desk every hour
asking what time the lounge would open. Just then the
phone rang again. This time, the manager took the call.
Sure enough, it was the same businessman, calling again
with the same question about what time the lounge
would open. The manager said, "Look here! The night
clerk tells me that you have been a nuisance all night
long, asking the same question. I am telling you for the
last time, the lounge will be open at 9:00 A.M. You can't
get in 'til then." To which the businessman replied, "Get
in? I don't want to get *in*; I want to get *out*!"

In our world today, a lot of people feel trapped like
that, and sadly they think that all they can do is just sit
there. Psychologists tell us that as long as we live, there
are two kinds of desires working within us, battling for
our allegiance. One is the desire to give up and quit on
life, to throw in the towel and congeal into some final
self. The other is the desire to keep on moving forward,
to keep on striving, to keep on learning, to keep on growing. And this is the calling of every Christian. This is the
desire that keeps us young in spirit and beautifully alive.
We must be constantly on guard against congealing. Or
in other words, "You can't just sit there!"

This is clearly what the call to discipleship is all
about—that it's not enough to just sit there, that the key
to life is to stand up and follow Jesus. Frederick
Buechner, in his book *Wishful Thinking: A Theological
ABC* ([New York: Harper & Row, 1973], p. 62), expressed
it so well as he described those early disciples.

> The first ministers were the twelve disciples. There is no
> evidence that Jesus chose them because they were
> brighter or nicer than other people. In fact the New
> Testament record suggests that they were continually

missing the point, jockeying for position, and when the chips were down, interested in nothing so much as saving their own skins. Their sole qualification seemed to have been their initial willingness to rise to their feet when Jesus said, "Follow me."

Their song was not so much "Lord, We Are Able," as it was "Lord, We Are *Available.*"

Now, what we learn from Simon, Andrew, James, and John is this: If you want to be available to follow Christ and to serve him and to be his disciple, you can't just "sit there." Let me show you what I mean with three thoughts.

First of All, Don't Just Sit There in Defeat

Before Jesus came along, that is exactly what those early disciples were doing. They felt defeated. I mean, what could they do? They didn't have the power to take on the Roman army. They didn't have the power to take on the Temple authorities. So they just wallowed in a spirit of defeat until Jesus came and delivered them.

Phillip Childs, a pastor with Parakletos Ministries in Decatur, Georgia, tells an intriguing story about a class of fourth graders in a public elementary school. The children were hard at work. The ten-year-old students were furiously writing, filling their pages with a list of "I Can'ts": "I can't kick the soccer ball past second base." "I can't do long division with more than three numbers." "I can't get Debbie to like me." Their pages were full, and they showed no signs of letting up.

Every student was writing his or her "I Can't" list. The teacher was also doing the same: "I can't get John's mother to come for a teacher conference." "I can't get my daughter to put gas in the car." "I can't get Alan to use words rather than fists." Why were they dwelling on the negative instead of writing the more positive "I Can" statements? Soon, the answer came.

The teacher stood up and said, "Okay, children, let's do it!" The children ran forward and put all of their "I Can't" lists into a shoe box. The teacher then grabbed a shovel and the shoe box and marched outside. The students followed close behind. They walked to the farthest corner of the school yard, and, one by one, they all took turns with the shovel. They were digging a grave!

When the grave was ready, thirty-one ten-year-olds stood there as their teacher placed the shoe box at the bottom of the hole. They covered it with dirt, and then the teacher said, "Boys and girls, please join hands and bow your heads." They did, and the teacher gave the eulogy.

> Friends, we are gathered here today to honor the memory of "I Can't." While he was here with us on earth he touched the lives of everyone, some more than others. We have provided "I Can't" with a final resting place and a headstone that contains his epitaph. He is survived by his brothers and sisters, "I Can," "I Will," and "I'm Going to Right Away." They are not as well known as their famous relative and are certainly not as strong and powerful yet. Perhaps some day, with your help, they will make an even bigger mark on the world. May "I Can't" rest in peace and may everyone present pick up their lives and move forward in his absence. Amen. (Phillip B. Childs, "The I Can't Funeral," *North Texas United Methodist Reporter* 31 [January 22, 1999]: 1)

What a great moment this was. These students would never forget this. But they weren't through yet. The group went back to the classroom and had cookies and popcorn and fruit juice. The teacher cut a large tombstone from brown paper. She wrote the words "I Can't" at the top and "Rest in Peace" at the bottom, and then she wrote the date. She hung the tombstone on the bulletin board for the rest of the year, and on those rare occasions when a student would feel defeated and say "I can't," the teacher would simply point to the "Rest in Peace" sign. The student would then remember that "I Can't" was dead and buried, and he or she would then resolve to try harder.

Jesus would like this story, I believe, because that is what he was saying to those first disciples: "You can *do* it." I will help you. Don't just sit there in defeat. Come on now. Get up and follow me." The apostle Paul would probably like this story too, because one of his most famous quotes says it all: "I can do all things through [Christ] who strengthens me" (Philippians 4:13).

The point is clear: The choice is ours. We can wallow in defeat, feel sorry for ourselves, and say, "We can't do anything about the complex problems that surround us"; or we can hear the call of Jesus and respond with courage and optimism and faith. To those early disciples long ago, and to you and me here and now, Jesus is saying, "Don't just sit there in defeat! Get up and come and follow me! You can *do* it. I will help you."

That's number one: Don't just sit there in defeat.

Second, Don't Just Sit There in Apathy

There's an old Smothers Brothers routine in which Tom seems worried. His brother, Dick, says to him, "What's the matter, Tom? You seem despondent."

"I am," replies Tom. "I'm worried about the state of American society."

"Well, what bothers you? Are you worried about poverty in our nation?" says Dick.

23

"No, that doesn't bother me," replies Tom.

"I see—Well, are you concerned about the danger of nuclear war?"

"No, that doesn't bother me."

"Are you upset about the use of drugs among our youth?"

"No, that doesn't bother me," says Tom.

"Well then," says Dick, "if you're not bothered by poverty, or war, or drugs, what *are* you worried about?"

And Tom responds: "I'm worried about our *apathy!*"

Well, Tom Smothers, in his unique way, may well have put his finger on one of the big problems of our time: apathy! This was also a big problem in Jesus' time. People felt down and out, with nowhere to turn, and so many of them just quit on life.

That is precisely what apathy is—it's quitting on life; it's just giving up and throwing in the towel. A punster friend of mine told me this week about the apathetic owl, who "just doesn't give a hoot anymore!" To be apathetic is to be uncaring, unconcerned, unexcited, unmoved, and untouched. It is the opposite of faith and hope, the opposite of love and commitment.

Last fall in Fort Lauderdale, Florida, a series of unusual messages appeared on billboards and buses. The agency in charge of the advertising campaign said that an anonymous donor was footing the bill. The messages were reported to be messages from God, and they caused quite a stir in town.

Here are some of the messages:

"Let's meet at my house Sunday before the game." (signed) God

"C'mon over and bring the kids." (signed) God

"What part of 'Thou Shalt Not' didn't you understand?" (signed) God

"We need to talk." (signed) God

"Keep using my name in vain and I'll make rush hour longer." (signed) God

"Loved the wedding; invite me to the marriage." (signed) God

"I love you—I love you—I love you." (signed) God

"Will the road you're now on get you to my place?" (signed) God

"Follow me." (signed) God

"Big bang theory? You have got to be kidding!" (signed) God

"My way is the highway." (signed) God

"You think it's hot *here*?" (signed) God

"Tell the kids I love them." (signed) God

"Have you read my No. 1 best-seller? There will be a test." (signed) God

"That 'love your neighbor' thing—I meant it!" (signed) God

That anonymous donor who put those messages up was trying in his own way to tell us what the New Testament says: "Don't just sit there in defeat and in apathy, get up and follow Jesus. You can *do* it! He will help you!"

Third and Finally, Don't Just Sit There in Indecision

There is an old joke that came out of the former Soviet Union many years ago about a Russian who stood on the street corner in Moscow and shouted, "Down with Khrushchev!" He was arrested on the spot and sent to prison for ten years. While he was in prison, he had a change of heart and came to see Nikita Khrushchev in a different light. The only problem was that while he had been in prison, the times had changed, and Khrushchev had been deposed, kicked out of office, and publicly denounced.

When the man was released, he went back to that same street corner in Moscow. He wanted to give a public testimony to his rehabilitation. This time, he shouted, "Hooray for Khrushchev!" and promptly got ten more years in prison, which only goes to show that "timing is everything!"

And this is one of the key things to notice in the Gospel of Mark. Jesus said, "Follow me," and immediately Simon, Andrew, James, and John dropped everything and followed him.

The question for us today is this: When is the best time to decide—to make up our minds—to follow Jesus? The answer is, Right now! Don't just sit there in defeat, in apathy, in indecision. The time is now. This is your moment. Get up now and follow Jesus. You can *do* it. He will help you. God is here, nearer than breathing, and God is calling you. Don't miss the call to discipleship!

✌ 2 ✌
Don't Miss . . .
The Spirit of Christ

Scripture: Matthew 5:13-16

A friend recently sent me a story about a mother who was preparing pancakes for her two sons one Saturday morning. Kevin and Ryan just loved pancakes. In fact, they loved their mom's pancakes so much that on this particular Saturday morning they began to argue (as brothers will do) over who would get the first pancake. Five-year-old Kevin and three-year-old Ryan were not only fussing; they were also pushing and shoving, trying, each one, to be first in line and get the first pancake.

Their mother saw the opportunity for a moral lesson, so she said, "Boys, boys! Calm down! I want to ask you a question. If Jesus were here with us this morning, what do you think he would say?" No answer. "Well," she continued, "I'll tell you what he would say. He would say, 'Please let my brother have the first pancake; I can wait.'"

In reply, five-year-old Kevin said, "Great idea, Mom!" and then he turned to his younger brother and said, "Ryan, *you* be Jesus!"

I love that story, not only because it's funny, but also because it is so typical of us. Most of us are convinced that the hard work of the gospel can and should be done, but we want somebody else to do it. We want great Sunday school classes for our children, our youth, and our adults, but we want somebody else to provide them. We want and expect to have a great choir, but we want somebody else to make it happen. We want somebody else to drive the bus for the youth, to look after the landscape, to help the poor, to visit the sick, to go on the mission work trip. We want the Spirit of Christ to be alive and well and evident in our church, our city, our world, but we want somebody else to do the work of Christ. Like five-year-old Kevin, we say, "*You* be Jesus—not me!"

The great nineteenth-century Danish theologian Søren Kierkegaard once told about the day he was walking down a street in Copenhagen and passed a shop that had a sign in the window. The sign read: "Pants Pressed Here." Kierkegaard said that he had walked in and begun to remove his trousers, when the owner of the shop said, "Sir, what on *earth* are you *doing*?" Kierkegaard said, "I'm removing my pants so you can press them." And the shop owner replied, "I don't press pants. I paint signs!" There's a sermon there, somewhere!

Kierkegaard, with his keen theological mind, said that the sermon there is this: One of the critical, ever-present problems we have within the Christian faith and within the Christian church is that some Christians are better "sign painters" than "pants pressers"; they "talk the talk" but want somebody else to "walk the walk." Think about it. We are pretty good at sign painting in the church. We have great signs all over the place—signs that read: "Everyone Welcome," "God Loves You, and So Do I," "Blessed Are the Peacemakers," "Blessed Are Those Who Hunger and Thirst for Righteousness," "Love Your Enemies and Pray for Those Who Persecute You," "The Biblical Guideline for Giving Is the Tithe," "Forgive Others as God in Christ Has Forgiven You," and "Be a Servant."

28

We have wonderful signs. It is clear to the whole world who we are and what we do and what we are all about. But sadly, too often (far too often), it ends up that we are much better at "painting the signs" than we are at actually "pressing the pants." In other words, we want somebody else to do the work. We want somebody else to "be Jesus" for the world.

Jesus was clearly a "pants presser." He had little patience with the "sign painters" of his day—those who *talked* a good game, but somehow never got around to doing the work of faith and hope and love. Remember how he said it in the Sermon on the Mount: "Not everyone who says to me, 'Lord, Lord,' will enter the kingdom of heaven, but only the one who does the will of my Father in heaven" (Matthew 7:21).

Have you ever noticed this in the Bible? In the Gospel of John, Jesus calls himself "the light of the world" (*see* 8:12; 9:5), but here in the Gospel of Matthew, Jesus calls *us*—you and me—"the light of the world" (5:14). What do we make of that? Simply this: that we, as Christians, are called to be reflectors of Christ's light; to be—by the power of his grace and the presence of his Holy Spirit—so tuned in to him, so committed to him, so positioned toward him that his light of love and forgiveness and hope and service just bounces off of us and spills out everywhere we go in this world. "You are the light of the world." You don't light a lamp and then put it under a basket. No! You share it with the world. Let your light so shine before others that they may see the work of Christ in you and give glory to your Father in heaven.

Let me ask you something. How are you personally doing with this? Can people see the light of Christ in you? Can people see the spirit of Jesus in you? Let me bring this closer to home by being more specific with three very basic questions. Here's number one.

First of All, Can People See in You Christ's Spirit of Forgiveness?

It was a cold and snowy night in January. On the floor of the hospital where Nurse Sue Kidd worked, things were pretty quiet. She stopped by room 712 to check on a new patient, Mr. Williams. Mr. Williams had been admitted with a heart attack, and he had seemed restless and anxious all evening. He perked up when the door to his room opened, but then looked disappointed to see Sue walk in. He was obviously expecting, hoping, for someone else. As Sue checked Mr. Williams's chart and asked about his condition, she sensed that he wanted very much to ask her something. Finally, with tears in his eyes, Mr. Williams asked Sue to call his daughter and tell her about his heart attack. His daughter was the only family that Mr. Williams had left now, and he seemed very anxious that she know of his condition.

Sue patted Mr. Williams's hand and promised to call his daughter right away. Before Sue left, Mr. Williams made another request: Could he have a piece of paper and a pencil? Sue took care of that and then went directly to the phone to call his daughter. When Sue reached Mr. Williams's daughter, Janie, with the news of her father's heart attack, she was startled by the young woman's reaction. Janie screamed, "No!" In a panic, she asked, "He's not dying, is he? Tell me he is not dying!"

In her distress, Janie blurted out that she and her father had not spoken in a year. They had gotten into a heated argument over Janie's boyfriend. It had been an ugly scene, with a lot of hostility and anger and tension. Janie and her father had not communicated since. Janie had stormed out and had refused to speak to her father. Her last words to her father had been "I hate you!" Of course, she hadn't meant that, and she had regretted having said it. All of this time, she had wanted forgiveness, and now a year and more had passed.

After reassuring Janie the best she could, Sue hung up the phone and began to pray. If only God would allow Mr. Williams and his daughter to reconcile! Her heart was so burdened by her phone conversation with Janie that Sue felt an urgent need to rush back to Mr. Williams's room to check on him. She found him unconscious, suffering from another heart attack. Within seconds, Sue's "Code 9" alerted the staff, and doctors and nurses filled the room in an attempt to save Mr. Williams; but it was too late. No amount of medical attention would restart his heart. He was gone.

As Sue walked into the hallway, she saw a doctor talking to a young woman. Shock and grief and panic mingled on the young woman's face. It was Mr. Williams's daughter, Janie. Sue ushered her into a lounge area and tried her best to comfort her, but Janie kept saying, "I never hated him. I loved him. I tried to get here in time to tell him, but now it's too late. Why was I so stubborn? Why was I so prideful? Now it's too late."

Janie wanted to see her father. Sue took her to his room. Janie leaned over her father's lifeless body and hugged him, and she cried painful tears.

Suddenly, Sue noticed something on Mr. Williams's nightstand: a piece of paper. Sue picked it up, and saw Janie's name was written at the top. Sue handed the note to Janie, and Janie read it out loud: "My dearest Janie, I'm sorry about that night. Please forgive me. Please know that I forgive you. Janie, I know that you love me. I know that you love me, and I love you with all my heart. Don't you forget that. (Signed) Daddy."

Where grief and shock and panic had contorted Janie's features and filled her eyes just moments before, now, though there was grief still, there was also peace. The nurse, Sue Kidd, slipped out of the room and headed straight to the telephone to call her father.

If we could go back in time to Golgotha and gaze upon the cross that held Jesus' dying body, we would see a sign mounted above his head. On this sign, we would see the words: "This man is the Son of God." If we could only see the back side of this sign, we might also find *these* words: "My dearest [and our own names would appear], I forgive you. I know that you love me, and I love you with all my heart. (Signed) Jesus." And there would be this P.S.: "By the way, this is how I want you to forgive one another: I want you to live daily in the spirit of reconciliation and forgiveness." (Adapted from *Dynamic Preaching* [September 1998]: 21-22.)

Well, how is it with you right now? Do you hold onto your grudges? Store up your hurts? Harbor your grievances? Look for a chance to "get 'em back"? Or—can people see in you Christ's amazing spirit of forgiveness?

Second, Can People See in You Christ's Spirit of Love?

A first-grade teacher collected some well-known proverbs and sayings. She gave her first graders the first half of each famous saying and asked them to come up with the rest. Here is what the kids came up with:

Better to be safe than—punch a fifth grader.
Strike while the—bug is close.
It's always darkest before—daylight savings time.
Never underestimate the power of—termites.
Don't bite the hand that—looks dirty.
A miss is as good as—a mister.
Where there is smoke—there's pollution.

If at first you don't succeed—get new batteries.
Laugh and the world laughs with you, cry and—you'll
  have to blow your nose.
A penny saved is—not much.
If you lie down with dogs—you will stink in the morn-
  ing.

Now, let me ask you something. How would you complete this saying: *"Love one another"*? Your answer
might be something like *"Love one another*—as God in
Christ has loved you"—in other words, unconditionally,
sacrificially, self-givingly, graciously, and compas-
sionately.

In Keith Miller's book *A Second Touch* ([Waco: Word
Books, 1967], pp. 63-64) there is a story about a busy
executive in an eastern city who was rushing to catch a
commuter train one morning. The executive had an
important meeting at the office, and he needed to make
this train in order to get there on time. Just as he was
about to board the train, he accidentally bumped into a
little boy who was carrying a boxed jigsaw puzzle. The
box went flying, and the pieces scattered everywhere.
What should he do? Should he stop and help the little
boy pick up the pieces? Or, should he get on the train?
He couldn't do both; there was not enough time! If he
stopped to help, he would miss the train and be late.
What should he do? What would *you* have done?

Well, the man stopped and helped the boy pick up the
puzzle as the train pulled out. The little boy watched
him closely with a kind of awe. The little boy said,
"Mister, you missed your train."

"I know," the man said.

"Will you be late for work?" the boy asked.

"Yes, but it was more important that I stop and help
you."

Then, the little boy said, "Mister, can I ask you a question?"

"Yes, of course."

"Mister, are you *Jesus?*"

Keith Miller wrote, "And for the moment, the man realized that—on that platform—he had been." That little boy saw the light of Jesus in that man's act of Christlike love.

Well, how is it with *you* these days? Can people see in you Christ's spirit of forgiveness? And can people see in you Christ's spirit of love?

Third and Finally, Can People See in You Christ's Spirit of Ministry?

In our church bulletin every Sunday, we print our mission statement. It reads like this: "St Luke's is a Christ-centered, servant church where every member has a ministry." That's a great statement. I love that! We are centered in Christ. We see ourselves as servants, not prima donnas, and there is a job here—a *ministry* here—for everybody.

Recently, one of our members was sitting in the sanctuary with his thirteen-year-old daughter. Church had not started yet, and the young woman asked her father how many members we have in our church. He answered, "Oh, I think we have about 7,500 members now."

The daughter replied, "How many ministers do we have?"

Her father started counting them on his fingers. "Well, let's see, there's Jim, and Lee, and Bill, and Carla, and Diana, and Mary, and Linda, and Amy—I don't know, probably eight or nine."

"No, Daddy," she said. "Look at this." She pointed to the mission statement and read it out loud: "St. Luke's is a Christ-centered, servant church, where every member has a ministry." And then she said, "*That* means we have *7,500* ministers!"

She was right, wasn't she? But let me ask you something: Have you found *your* ministry yet? Have you found your job here, in this world, yet? We have all kinds of jobs here. Some of them are technical and some of them call for special talent, but most of them require only willing hearts and willing hands. When Jesus called those early disciples to join him in ministry—don't miss this, now!—they were not professional clergypersons; they were not trained priests. No, they were simply regular folk with willing hands and willing hearts who just made themselves available, so that the light of Christ could reflect off of them. That's what we are called to do and to be—ready, willing, and available to do our best and to trust in God for the rest.

I have on my desk a benediction from India. It goes like this:

May the Lord disturb you and trouble you,
May the Lord set an impossible task before you,
And dare you to meet it.
May the Lord give you strength to do your best
And then—but only then—
May you be granted the Lord's Peace.

What does that mean? Simply this: The greatest satisfaction is in service. The greatest meaning is in ministry. The greatest joy is in reflecting the light of Jesus in this world. So the question for us to ask ourselves is this: Can people see in you and in me the light of Christ? It's not enough to say to those around us, "*You* be Jesus." The question is, Can people see in you and in me Christ's spirit of forgiveness, Christ's spirit of love, and Christ's spirit of ministry?

❧ 3 ❧

Don't Miss . . .
Having Your Eyes "*Christ*-ed"

Scripture: John 9:1-12

Recently, I ran across a fascinating list that carried this intriguing title: "Great Truths About Life That Little Children Have Learned." Let me share a few of these "great truths" with you.

"No matter how hard you try, you cannot baptize a cat."
"When your mom is mad at your dad, don't let her brush your hair."
"Never ask your three-year-old brother to hold a tomato—or an egg."
"You can't trust dogs to watch your food for you."
"Don't sneeze when somebody is cutting your hair."
"School lunches stick to the wall."
"You can't hide a piece of broccoli in a glass of milk."
"Never wear polka-dot underwear under white shorts—no matter how cute the underwear is."

Now, it is virtually certain that the children learned these "great truths" and came to these bold new insights after some dramatic, eye-opening experience in their own personal lives. Can't you just see, in your mind's eye, some children trying to baptize a cat, and learning full well from that experience that this is just not a good thing to do? The point is clear: A dramatic, personal, eye-opening experience can give us new insight, new perception, new vision.

On a much deeper level, and on a much more positive level, that's precisely what we discover in this amazing story in John 9. A man who has been blind since birth has a dramatic eye-opening experience with Jesus, and as a result he is completely and totally healed. He comes back from the pool of Siloam with 20/20 vision, able to see perfectly for the first time in his life. His transformation is so complete and so dramatic that he even looks a little different. The townspeople see him and say, "Hey, isn't that the blind beggar? He can see now. Is that *him*? No, it's just someone who looks like him. *Couldn't* be him," And the formerly blind man says, "It's *me*, all right. I am that man."

Remember the story with me.

One day as Jesus and his disciples were walking along together, they saw what they considered to be a pitiful sight: a man, who had been blind from birth, groveling and begging there in the gutter. To the disciples, this man made a sad, haunting picture as he crouched there, feeling around in the dirt for scraps of garbage; using his hands and arms to ward off the trampling, heedless crowds; wallowing in the dust and pleading—without much success—for help. Intrigued by this man's horrible plight, the disciples asked Jesus a difficult theological question: *Why* was this man born blind? Who sinned? Was it this man or his parents? Was it his fault? Or did someone in his family do something wrong to cause this?

There is an interesting theological point here. The religious leaders of Jesus' time had the mistaken notion that persons who were experiencing what was considered to be a hardship (including persons with physically disabling conditions) were in that circumstance because that person or one of his family members had sinned; it was believed that this was God's judgment upon them for their wrongdoings. So persons who were blind, or who could not walk, or who had the debilitating disease leprosy, or who were simply poor were looked down upon by society as sinners—as wicked people—and they were shunned. But Jesus didn't see them as sinners or as wicked people. He saw them as children of God, as persons of integrity and worth, as members of God's family, as his brothers and sisters, and he loved them, embraced them, enjoyed them, and healed them.

So in John 9, Jesus went over to the man who was blind to help him. Notice that when the disciples saw the blind man, they regarded him as an opportunity for a discussion; but when Jesus saw the man, he saw instead an opportunity to *do* something. The disciples wanted to debate the truth; Jesus chose to *reveal* the truth to all. The disciples wanted to give their energy to words; Jesus put *his* energy into action. The point is this: It's not enough to talk about it. What pleases God is when we *do* something about it.

This is the point Jesus was trying to teach us in John 9. Notice that Jesus spat upon the ground, made clay of the spittle, and then anointed the man's eyes with the clay. Now, if this seems repulsive to you, don't let it be. Saliva has long been a folk remedy. Ancient people believed strongly in its curative powers, and, in a sense, we still do. At least, our children do. For example, a child burns his finger, and into his mouth it goes; or a child scrapes her arm and wants Mom to kiss it and make it well.

In several translations of the Bible, John 9:6 says that after Jesus spat on the ground and made clay of the spittle, he then "anointed the man's eyes with the clay" (RSV). Now, the single most important word in this whole passage is the word *anointed*. The word that the original Greek text uses here for "anointed" or "anoints" is the same word it uses for the word *Christ*, which, of course, means "the Anointed One." Don't miss this! Jesus *anoints* the man's eyes, which, put another way, means that he "Christs" the man's eyes! Isn't that beautiful? He "Christs" the man's eyes! Now, let me ask you something. "Would you like to have *your* eyes *Christed?*"

Recall the rest of the story. After anointing the man's eyes with the clay, Jesus sent him to wash in the pool of Siloam. The man went, washed away the clay, and came back seeing! The neighbors were amazed. They couldn't believe it. They asked the man who had been blind how this had happened, and he replied that the man called Jesus had healed him: "Jesus gave me my sight."

And there was great joy in the city, and they all lived happily ever after, right? No, not quite! The Pharisees, the watchdogs of religion, got wind of this story, and they came out fuming, upset about the whole business, because for one thing, they were suspicious of *everything* Jesus did. And on top of this, this healing had happened on the Sabbath day—a blatant violation of the Pharisees' rigid rules. "Jesus made clay—he healed—on the Sabbath, and this is strictly forbidden. We can't have this!"

So the Pharisees came out with the fervor of Mayberry Deputy Barney Fife to investigate. They interrogated the healed man's parents and scared them out of their wits, and then they interrogated the man who had been healed, and he gave them a classic and powerful response that has resounded across the centuries. He said, "This one thing I know: Once I was blind, but now I see." You see, this man (like most people) was a pragmatist. Look at what he was saying in response to the Pharisees' hardline questioning! "I don't know about all of that. I don't know about rules or regulations or restrictions—but I *do* know results when I see them. This one thing I do know.

Once I was blind, but now I see." The Pharisees were defeated by this argument, and they knew it. So they did what people often do when they feel insecure or have no moral power: they turned to force. They kicked him out. They cast him out of the synagogue. They excommunicated him. They pushed him out.

Now, this set the stage for one of the most beautiful moments in all of Scripture. Jesus heard about it. He heard that the Pharisees cast the man out, and Jesus went to find him. Aware of the man's newfound trouble, Jesus came to him. Jesus came to help. That's the good news, isn't it? It is that when we are in trouble, Jesus comes to help! And when the two came face-to-face, Jesus said to the man, "Do you believe in me, the Son of God?" And the healed man replied, "Lord, I believe." And then the man worshiped Jesus (John 9:35-38, paraphrased)!

Isn't this a great story? It is so packed with the stuff of life. There is so much here—blindness and sight, sickness and healing, prejudice and love, fear and faith, rejection and acceptance, defeat and victory. But there is one question that explodes out of this Gospel story and addresses itself directly and personally to you and to me, namely this: Have your eyes been *Christ*-ed? Can you see with the vision of our Lord? Have your eyes been anointed with the spirit of Christ? Let me break this down a bit and be more specific.

First, When Your Eyes Have Been "*Christ*-ed," It Changes the Way You See Yourself

Listen! You were born blind, and so was I. Babies are born spiritually "blind." Now, please don't misunderstand me. I love little babies. They are wonderful! They represent God's greatest miracle, the miracle of birth, and as it's been said, they represent God's affirmation that life should go on. But the truth is that they are born blinded by the cataracts of selfishness. They see every person as someone who exists solely for their benefit and comfort. That's the way babies are. They come into the world screaming: Do something for me! Feed me, love me, hold me, burp me, change me, rock me—in that order, in the reverse order, in any order you like and at any time you like, as long as it's right now! Throughout infancy and childhood, into the teen years, and, sadly, even into adulthood for some, it's ME, ME, ME. Take care of me, do for me, cater to me, please me, give to me, pamper me.

But then Jesus brings us up short, because time and again in the Gospels, Jesus makes it very clear that one of the things that blinds us most is selfishness, and the only cure for it is to have our eyes Christ-ed. Bishop Kenneth Shamblin used to say that *conversion* is moving from "That belongs to me!" to "I belong to that!" That's what it means to have your eyes Christ-ed—to move from selfish vision to service vision, to move from "Do something for me" to "Let me *do* and *be* for God and for others."

Let me ask you something. Have you had your eyes Christ-ed? Can you see beyond your own selfish desires? Can you see yourself not as one to be selfishly pampered, but as one committed to be God's servant in this world?

Second, When Your Eyes Have Been "*Christ*-ed," It Changes the Way You See Other People

A friend recently told me a powerful story about a mother who took her children to a crowded restaurant one day. The woman's six-year-old son asked if he could say grace. He prayed, "God is great, and God is good; let us thank him for our food. And God, I would thank you even more if Mom gets us ice cream for dessert. And liberty and justice for all! Amen!" Along with the laughter from the other customers nearby, the woman at the very next table grumbled loudly: "That's what's *wrong* with this country! Kids today don't even know how to pray. The very idea—asking God for ice cream! Why, I *never!*"

Hearing this, the little six-year-old boy burst into tears and asked his mother, "Did I do it wrong? I'm sorry. Is God mad at me?" The little boy's mother pulled him over onto her lap. She hugged him tightly and assured him that he had done a terrific job with his prayer, and that God was certainly not mad at him. Just then an elderly gentleman walked over to the table. He winked at the little boy, and said, "I know God really well. We visit every day, and I happen to know that God loved your prayer. It may have been the best one he has heard all day."

"Really?" the little boy asked.

"Cross my heart," said the man. Then he leaned over and whispered into the little boy's ear. Pointing at the woman at the next table who had made the remark that started the whole thing, he said, "Too bad *she* never asks God for ice cream. A little ice cream is good for the soul, sometimes."

Naturally, the boy's mother ordered ice cream for her children at the end of the meal. The six-year-old stared at his ice cream for a moment, and then he did something that no one in the restaurant that day will ever forget. He picked up his ice cream sundae and without a word walked over and placed it in front of the woman at the next table. With a big smile, he said to her, "Here, this is for you. Ice cream is good for the soul, sometimes, and my soul is good already!" The people in the restaurant applauded, and somewhere in heaven, Jesus was smiling because that little boy had already learned how to look at others with the eyes of sacrificial love. Sight—true sight—is always a matter of the heart, *not* the eyes.

When our eyes have been Christ-ed, we see with our hearts, and we realize what Jesus taught long ago: that we are all in this together, that we are all persons for whom Christ came and died. When our eyes are anointed with the Spirit of Christ, then we see people differently. We see them as part of God's family, and we accept them and embrace them and help them and treat them with respect and love. That's what it means to have *Christ*-ed eyes. When our eyes have been Christ-ed, it changes the way we see ourselves, and changes the way we see other people.

Third and Finally, When Your Eyes Have Been *"Christ*-ed," It Changes the Way You See God

There's something fascinating here in John 9. Don't miss this now. Notice the way the healed man refers to Jesus. Notice the growth. There is a magnificent progression here as he sees more and more clearly. Look at this.

First, he refers to Jesus as a man. He says, "The man Jesus did this for me" (*see* verse 11).

Next, he calls Jesus a prophet. He says, "To be able to do this he must be a prophet" (*see* verse 17).

Then, in that intimate moment at the end, he sees Jesus as the Son of God, the "Son of Man" (verses 35-36).

And finally, he claims Jesus as the Lord of his life (verse 38).

Did you notice? The closer the man got to Jesus, the more time he spent with Jesus, the clearer he saw God! And that's the way it works for us too, because, you see, that's what it means to have *Christ*-ed eyes. Please don't miss that!

4

Don't Miss . . .
The Gift of Amazing Grace

Scripture: John 4:7-29

I have a minister friend named Tom who does a fascinating thing each month. Even though he has an extremely busy schedule (because he serves as pastor of one of the finest churches in our nation), he still takes the time each month to go down to the homeless shelter in his city to work in the soup kitchen.

After the people at the shelter have been fed, Tom will then invite them to join him in a service of Holy Communion, and many of them will come with him to the little chapel in the shelter and join in the Sacrament of the Lord's Supper. They have shared soup together in the soup kitchen, and then they come to share the bread and the cup together at the altar in the chapel.

One day during one of these Communion services, Tom had an unforgettable experience that he loves to tell about. As he was moving down the altar, serving Communion, he came to a man kneeling there who looked as though he had been out on the streets for quite a while. The man looked up at Tom and whispered, "Skip me."

"What? Pardon me?" Tom said.

In a louder whisper, the man said again, "Skip me."

"Why?" Tom asked.

"Because," the man said, "I'm not worthy."

Tom said to him, "Neither am I." And then Tom

added, "I'll tell you what. I'm going to serve Communion to these other people. Then, I'm going to come back and serve Communion to you, and then I would like you to serve it to me."

The man blinked in amazement and said to Tom, "Father, is that *legal*?"

"Yes, it's legal; it's beautiful, and that's what we are going to do!" Tom answered.

Tom went on down the altar and served all of the other people kneeling there. And then he came back to the reluctant man and said, "What's your name?"

The man replied, "Josh."

Tom placed the elements of the Lord's Supper before him and said, "Josh, here is the body of Christ, and here is the blood of Christ given for you. Eat this and drink this in the remembrance that Christ came for you and Christ died for you. Amen."

Josh blinked back the tears in his eyes, and he received Holy Communion. Then, Tom knelt and handed Josh the trays of bread and wine and said, "Now, you serve me."

Josh nervously took the trays, and again he asked, "Father, are you sure this is legal?"

"Yes, it's legal. Just do it," Tom replied.

Josh's eyes were darting from side to side as he looked over this shoulder and then the other, as if he expected at any moment the police, the FBI, the CIA, or the pope to come rushing in to arrest him.

Finally, he held the trays toward Tom, and as Tom received the Sacrament, Josh muttered, "Body—blood—for you. Hang in there!"

Tom said later, "Of all the Communion rituals I have ever heard, I don't recall the words "hang in there" in any of them. But at that moment for me, Holy Communion had never been more "holy."

"Josh walked out of the shelter that day with an extra

"spring in his step," and it was reported that everywhere he went, he said, "You won't *believe* what I did today!" In fact, the story became so widespread that from that day Josh became known on the streets as "The Rev," which of course was short for "The Reverend."

What a remarkable story this is, the story of grace, love, acceptance, forgiveness, reconciliation, bridge building—and Holy Communion. That story reminds me of the powerful passage of Scripture in John 4 regarding Jesus' encounter with the Samaritan woman at the well. Consider the similarities.

- Both incidents involved a moment of amazing grace and Holy Communion.
- Like Josh, the Samaritan woman felt unworthy and wasn't very sure that this encounter with Jesus was legal.
- Like Josh (in all probability), the Samaritan woman was accustomed to being sneered at, talked about, looked down upon, and turned away in society.

The Samaritan woman had had five husbands. At the time of her encounter with Jesus, she was unmarried but living with a man, prompting some scholars to suggest that she was known in her town as promiscuous and a harlot. Other scholars surmise that the Samaritan woman had been a victim of society because in those days, in that patriarchal society, it was the husband who requested and received a divorce—meaning that this woman in one way or another had been "discarded" five times.

Whatever the case, one thing is clear: This Samaritan woman was an outcast, and she had a bad reputation. And still, Jesus reached out to her with love and compassion.

Remember the story with me.

The Bible tells us that the time was around noon. This means that it must have been incredibly hot out there at that desert well at midday. Jesus had been walking in the heat for some time. The disciples had gone into the near-by village of Sychar to buy some food. Jesus was resting at the well, probably sitting in the small shade the well could provide.

While the Master was waiting there, a woman of Samaria came out to the well. By the standards of the day, she had many "strikes" against her. First of all, she was a Samaritan. The Jews and Samaritans were enemies and had been for four hundred years.

Second, she was a woman with a bad reputation—bad to the point where she probably had no real choice but to walk to this particular well, which was half a mile from the city, to get her water, because the women of Sychar likely had banished her from the village well.

Most people would have turned away from this "labeled" woman for fear of guilt by association, but not Jesus. Instead, he asked her to share some water with him. She was astonished at this request, and in her amazement she said, "You are a Jew; I'm a Samaritan; you mean you want to associate with me? You actually want to share water with me? Is this *legal*? Don't you know who I am?" (John 4:9, paraphrased).

Jesus went on not only to share water with her, but also conversation (and this too was unheard of). And in this time of communication, Jesus shared with this Samaritan woman the good news of who he was and what he could do for her—how he could give her living water, forgiveness, and new life. And the woman got so excited that she tossed her water jar aside and ran back to town to tell everyone who would listen that she had met the Christ!

I love this story for a number of reasons. Let me lift up

three elements in this great story that underscore three main points of the Christian gospel. Are you ready? Here's number one.

First of All, Jesus Reached Out to the Samaritan Woman; He Took the Initiative

This story in John 4 demonstrates what is known as "prevenient grace," or, better put, "amazing grace." The woman at the well had done nothing to merit Jesus' attention, nothing to earn his forgiveness, and nothing to deserve his love; instead, these were freely given, and Jesus took the initiative in offering them. He sought her out. He reached out to her.

Some years ago, I had a friend named Ron. Ron was going through a tough time. His daughter was having a hard time growing up. She had become surly, rebellious, arrogant, and difficult. It was one crisis after another with her. She was constantly in trouble, but Ron never wavered. He kept on praying that his daughter would someday soon "get her act together," and he kept on loving her and forgiving her.

When Ron's daughter was sixteen, she ran away from home. All kinds of hurtful reports came back about the lifestyle she was living, but no one could pinpoint exactly where she was. Finally, Ron got word that somebody had seen her in a nearby city. Ron went to look for her. He asked me to go with him.

I'll never forget that experience, or the look on Ron's face as we searched all day and into the night for his prodigal daughter. Written large on his face was this look of intense urgency and deep love, as we went into one dive after another, one bar after another, one teenage hangout after another. And everywhere we went, Ron would do the same thing. He would show people a picture of his daughter and ask if anyone had seen her. No luck! They either hadn't seen her or they weren't talking. And everywhere we went that day, Ron stuck a picture of his wife and himself near the door. With the picture was a note that read:

Kathy, all is forgiven! We love you! Please come home! (Signed) Mom and Dad

We didn't find Kathy that day, but two weeks later she did come home, dirty, disheveled, and hungry, but okay. She said, "I couldn't believe my eyes. I walked into this bar one night and saw my mom and dad's picture, and that note. And then, I went to another place, and another, and another, and everywhere I went, there was my mom and dad's picture—and that note, forgiving me and pleading with me to come home. And that night, for the first time in my life, I realized how much my mom and dad love me. I have hurt them so many times. I have broken their hearts so many times, and still they came looking for me; still they love me."

Where did Ron and his wife learn to love like that, to reach out like that, to forgive like that? *You* know, don't you? They learned it from Jesus, the One who said to the woman at the well, "I know all about you. I know about your sins. I know about your past. I know about your sordid reputation; and I still love you, I still value you, I still care about you, I still forgive you, and I want to help you make a new start with your life."

Jesus reached out to that Samaritan woman. He didn't wait. He took the initiative. That's one of the greatest things about Christian love. It doesn't wait around to be asked. It seeks people out. It reaches out with love and grace, with forgiveness and reconciliation. That's number one: Jesus reached out to the woman. He took the initiative. And you know, he is reaching out with love and forgiveness to you and me right now.

Second, Jesus Broke Down the Barriers That Divide People

There is a gospel song that has these words: "Jesus, Jesus, Jesus! There's just something about that name." Indeed, there is. The name *Jesus*, of course, means "Savior" or "the Lord's Helper." But in addition (don't miss this now!), the name *Jesus* is the Greek form of the Hebrew name *Joshua*. And do you remember who Joshua was? He was the wall breaker. As the words of the spiritual go, "Joshua fit the battle of Jericho—and the walls come a-tumblin' down." So, Jesus is well named, because he too is a wall breaker. As Ephesians 2:14 puts it, "He has made [us] into one and has broken down the dividing wall, that is, the hostility between us."

We see that so vividly here in John 4. Look at the barriers Jesus knocks down here: the walls that separate men and women; the walls that separate Jews and Samaritans; the walls that separate a respected rabbi and a notorious outcast; all of those walls come tumbling down because of Jesus' love and grace and forgiveness.

Recently in a place of business I saw a sign that read: "To err is human; to forgive is not our policy." Some people live like that, and it is so sad. In Jesus' day, the Jews and Samaritans lived like that.

Prejudice, bigotry, vengeance, harshness toward other people—all of these are sinful. They are dividing walls. They are spiritual poisons. Think about it like this. If you put a plastic covering over a plant, the rain and sun can't get to it, and the plant will wither and wilt and ultimately will die. Prejudice and bigotry and hatred are like that plastic covering, and we are like the plant; we can't

51

be spiritually healthy until that plastic covering is removed.

Let me ask you something: Has someone hurt you? Do you feel estranged or alienated or "walled off" from anyone? Do you have bitterness in your heart toward any other person? If so, go fix that! Don't wait around anymore, don't put it off any longer. For your sake, for their sake, for God's sake—go fix it! Ask God to go with you. Ask God to be within you, and with God's help and power, go set it right. Go break down that dividing wall of hostility.

If we want to serve Christ, if we want to do his work, if we want to live in his Spirit, then our calling is to join forces with him in knocking down the dividing walls of pride, prejudice, and hostility, and in building bridges of love, understanding, acceptance, and forgiveness.

First, Jesus took the initiative and reached out to the Samaritan woman, and second, he broke down the barriers that divide people.

Third and Finally, He Changed Her Life

Talk about change: Someone has said that the woman at the well became the first missionary! She was so excited about what she had found in Christ that she forgot her water jar and ran to tell the people in town that she had discovered the Messiah.

But notice this: At first, the Samaritan woman was suspicious of Jesus. She was remote and standoffish and flippant. She saw him as the enemy, the opponent, the adversary. But then, at the end of their visit, she saw him as the Messiah.

What made the difference? How did the redemption happen? What caused the dramatic change? It didn't happen through criticism or fussing or nagging or harsh judgment. It happened because Jesus loved her, accepted her, included her, respected her, cared about her.

When will we ever learn this? Change does not come from harshness. It comes from unconditional love! If you want to convert somebody, don't fuss at them; *love* them! Reflecting on his own life, noted writer Anthony de Mello put it beautifully when he wrote these poignant words:

> I was a neurotic for years. I was anxious and depressed and selfish. Everyone kept telling me to change. I resented them, and I agreed with them, and I wanted to change, but simply couldn't no matter how hard I tried. What hurt the most was that, like the others, my best friend kept insisting that I change. So I felt powerless and trapped.
>
> Then, one day, he said to me, "Don't change. I love you just as you are." Those words were music to my ears: "Don't change. Don't change. Don't change. . . . I love you as you are." I relaxed. I came *alive*. And suddenly I changed! Now I know that I couldn't really change until I found someone who would love me whether I changed or not. Is this how you love me, God? (*Song of the Bird* [Garden City, N.Y.: Image Books, 1987], pp. 67-68)

Indeed, it is! And that's what Jesus shows us in John 4. Jesus took the initiative that day and reached out to the Samaritan woman at the well. And today, in the same way, Jesus reaches out to you and me. That day, Jesus broke down the walls and barriers that divide people, and today he wants us to join him in that sacred ministry of peacemaking.

And with his unconditional love, Jesus changed that woman's life that day. The point is, today—right now!— Jesus can change your life and mine. He knows all about us, and he loves us still, and he comes offering forgiveness and reconciliation to you and me. Don't miss that! Don't miss the wonderful gift of Jesus' "amazing grace."

❧ 5 ❧

Don't Miss . . .
The Power of the Cross

Scripture: 1 Corinthians 1:18-25

Recently, I ran across a list of fascinating questions. Even though the list sports the bold title "Deep Thoughts," I really think the questions are designed more to make us laugh than to make us think. Let me share some of these with you and show you what I mean:

For example, question number one asks: "Isn't it a bit unsettling that doctors call what they do 'practice'? Not to even *mention* lawyers!"

Or how about this one: "When sign makers go on strike, is there anything written on their signs?"

I love this one: "Why do they lock gas station bathrooms? Are they afraid somebody will get in there and clean them up?"

And here's one to really think about: "What's another word for *synonym*?"

And this one: "If a parsley farmer is sued, can they garnish his wages?"

And another: "Is it okay for a vegetarian to eat animal crackers?"

But my favorite question of all is this last one: "If a man speaks in the forest and there is no woman there to hear him, is he still wrong?"

Now, this list of fascinating questions reminds me of an old story that comes out of World War II, in which a young soldier asked a poignant question in the heat of battle. There was heavy shelling and bombardment going on that day on the front lines. In the midst of this horrendous barrage of firepower, an American GI was stunned (to say the least) when another American soldier suddenly jumped into his foxhole with him. Quarters were tight as the two young men tried their best to keep down and avoid enemy fire.

All of a sudden, the new occupant of the foxhole noticed something shiny in the dirt. He picked it up. It was a cross. Quickly, he rubbed the dust off of the front of the cross, and then he turned to his newfound American friend in the foxhole. With complete seriousness, he said, "How in the world do you make this thing work?"

Now, this young, inquiring soldier, in his fear and desperation, was obviously confused. For as *we* know, we don't make the cross "work." The cross is not some electronic gadget that we turn on and off as need requires. It is not some magic lamp that we rub on a whim to get our personal wishes granted. The cross is not some good-luck charm like a four-leaf clover or a rabbit's foot. (By the way, every time I see a rabbit's foot, I think about how it wasn't so lucky for the rabbit, and he had four of them!)

But, give that young soldier some credit. He didn't quite get it, but he did realize that there is great power in the cross. He was right about that, wasn't he? There is great power in the cross. Do you know why? Because the cross is the message of God, the truth of God, the victory of God, the gospel of God, the love of God, acted out in human history. This is what the apostle Paul was talking about in 1 Corinthians when he said, "For the message about the cross is foolishness to those who are perishing, but to us who are being saved it is the power of God" (1:18).

Some years ago, someone asked Anna Pavlova, the

great Russian dancer, what she meant by a certain dance she performed. "What was she saying in that dance?" I love her answer. She said, "If it could be said in words, there would be no need to dance it." Precisely! Certain truths are too big for words. They have to be dramatized. They have to be acted out. And that's why the cross and the Resurrection are so important to us. There, on the Old Rugged Cross of Good Friday, and there at the empty tomb of Easter morning, God dramatized his message. God acted it out for us. And now this symbol, the sign of the cross, serves as a constant and powerful reminder of God's truth for us, God's will for us, God's love for us.

Now, with three thoughts, allow me to underscore why the cross is the central focus of our Christian faith and our number one symbol.

First of All, the Cross Is Central Because It Reminds Us of the Ugliness of Sin

When we look at the cross, of course we think of God's love and grace, but also we cannot miss that it was sin that nailed Jesus to the cross. The cross reminds us that we are sinners. It reminds us of how much we need a Savior. In this modern age, we don't take sin very seriously anymore. Not too many years ago the villains of our time turned us off, but now we make them our celebrities. But the cross is a reminder to us of how destructive sin can be.

During World War II, the famous writer Antoine de Saint-Exupéry was called back into active duty with the French Air Force. On July 31, 1944, while flying an unarmed observation mission, his plane was shot down by a young German flyer, and the great French writer was killed.

Now, it just so happened that the young German pilot

who shot Saint-Exupéry down had been in the process of writing his doctoral dissertation on the life and works of the great French writer Saint-Exupéry. The German was an avid admirer of the Frenchman and almost worshiped him. When the German learned who it was that he had shot down, he suffered a breakdown and had to be put into a psychiatric hospital. All he could do was repeat over and over and over, "I have killed my master! I have killed my master!"

It seems to me that this true story out of World War II is a capsule of one of the great tragedies of life: namely, that sometimes we unwittingly kill what we love—our marriages, our families, our friendships, our own selves, and our relationship with God.

I once heard a young woman say to me through her tears, "Jim, I'm so ashamed. I don't know what gets into me, but sometimes I crucify people I love with cruel words. I destroy what I ought to value most!" Now, blow that up a bit, and you have the tragedy of Holy Week. Blow that up a bit, and toss in some "cloak and dagger" tactics, some calculated cunning, some selfish scheming, and you have the ingredients that produced Good Friday, Golgotha, "the place of the skull." We cannot look at the cross without remembering the sordid sinfulness that conspired to crucify Jesus.

First, the cross is central because it reminds us of the ugliness of sin.

Second, the Cross Is Central Because It Reminds Us of the Beauty of Sacrifice

Our modern world urges us to think only of ourselves, to look out for number one, to give our energies only to what we want. But then the cross "jumps up" to remind us again of the power and beauty of sacrifice.

Noted professor Fred Craddock tells about being snowed in while on a speaking engagement in Winnipeg, Canada. Three feet of snow! His host called and said, "Of course, we have had to cancel your lecture this morning. Everything in the city is shut down. In fact, I can't even get out of my driveway to take you to breakfast. However, there is a little café about two blocks away if you get hungry enough to brave this blizzard."

Fred Craddock bundled up the best that he could, shoveled his way out of his motel room, and made his way through the deep snow and harsh winter winds to the little café. It was crowded and noisy with stranded travelers. Dr. Craddock took a seat. The owner of the café, wearing a greasy apron, came over to take his order. He was a large, burly man, gruff and loud, with tattoos on his arms. This conversation took place.

"What'll you have?"

"May I see a menu?"

"Whattaya *mean, menu*? We have *soup!* That's *all! Soup!* Take it or leave it!"

"Soup—that's *just* what I was going to order. Soup and coffee. I *love* that for breakfast!"

A few minutes later when the soup arrived, it was indescribably horrible, some sort of unrecognizable gray broth that looked just awful, and it tasted even worse. Dr. Craddock took one small sip and put his spoon down. He could not eat it at all. Just about then the door to the café opened, and a blast of frigid wind swept through. An older woman came in, all bundled up, but obviously very cold. The temperature outside was far below zero. The woman's face was red and chapped. She was trembling and shuddering from the cold. She sat down at the only seat left in the café. The burly owner walked over to take her order.

"Cup of coffee, please," she said.

"Look, lady," the owner retorted. "You can't drink coffee in here! Order a meal or you have to leave!"

"But I just want coffee. It's so cold outside. Couldn't I just sit here for a few minutes to warm up?"

"No way!" said the owner gruffly. "Order a meal now, or get out!"

The attention of everyone in the café was riveted on that scene. The older woman's eyes began to moisten with tears as she stood to leave, when suddenly a voice boomed out from the other side of the restaurant. "If *she* leaves, we *all* leave!"

"That's just *fine* with *me!*" the owner shouted back. Immediately, every person in the café stood up and started for the door.

"All right! All right!" the owner said. "You win. You made your point. Come on back. The lady can stay, and she can have her coffee, and some soup. She can stay as long as she wants, and it's all on the house."

Everybody cheered! The patrons all happily returned to their places, and things got back to normal. Fred Craddock said that as he sat back down, all he could hear was the slurping of soup, and he thought to himself: *If* they *can handle it, so can* I! So, he picked up his spoon and dipped it into the gray soup. Amazingly, somehow it tasted different now. It was pretty good soup! Why, it tasted like something very familiar. "It tasted," he said, "like bread and wine!" It tasted like bread and wine now, because they had just experienced a Holy Communion on that cold morning in that little café in Canada.

You see, when people stand tall for what is right, there is Holy Communion. When people come together for justice and band together in love—when people sacrifice for one another—there is Holy Communion.

That's what the symbol of the cross is about—sacrifice, going out on a limb for one another. That's what

Jesus did for us at Golgotha. He died that we might live. He sacrificed for us, for you and me. Sacrifice: This is the spirit in which God wants us to live.

The cross reminds us of the ugliness of sin and the beauty of sacrifice.

Third and Finally, the Cross Is Central Because It Reminds Us of the Power of Salvation

In many churches today, it has become something of a tradition at Easter and at memorial or funeral services to sing the song "Hymn of Promise," written by Natalie Sleeth, a wonderful and prolific writer of Christian music. She wrote this hymn for her husband, the late Dr. Ronnie Sleeth, who was an outstanding professor of preaching. From the date of the diagnosis of his illness to his death were just twenty-one days, and Natalie wrote this hymn of promise for him before he died. Look at these powerful words from the last stanza:

In our death, a resurrection; at the last, a victory,
Unrevealed until its season, something God alone can see.

Natalie had her own set of health problems. For several years she battled a debilitating disease that ultimately took her life. Before she died, she wrote a beautiful statement for her grandchildren. She told them of how she began to realize that she was growing older and that her body was beginning to wear out. She told her grandchildren that she had talked to God about this and had asked God to help her. God had heard her and said, "My child, when I made the world and filled it with people, I had a plan. I wanted my people to have life as long as they could, but not forever on this earth because then my world would be too full with no room for anybody. I planned it so that when it was time to leave the earth, my people would come and live with me in heaven where there is no pain or sadness or sickness or anything bad."

Natalie told her grandchildren that at this point, she said softly to God, "Is my time to come and live with you getting closer?" And God said, "Yes, but don't be afraid, because I will always be with you, and I will always take care of you." Natalie said to God, "But, I will miss my family and my friends, and they will miss me!" And God said, "Yes, but I will comfort them and turn their tears into joy, and they will remember you with happiness and be glad of your life among them."

So, slowly, Natalie began the journey to heaven, and day by day she drew nearer and nearer to God. In the distance, she said, she could see light and hear beautiful music and feel happiness that she had never known before. And as she moved toward the gates of heaven and into the house of God, she said her last words: "It's good! It's good! It's good!"

This is the good news of our faith and the power of salvation—that nothing, not even death, can separate us from the love of God in Christ Jesus our Lord. The cross is central in our faith because it dramatically reminds us of the ugliness of sin, the beauty of sacrifice, and the power of salvation. And, consequently, the cross is central because it challenges us to live in the spirit of penitence, in the spirit of love, and in the spirit of trust.

May Jesus keep us near the cross!

❧ 6 ❧

Don't Miss . . .
The Great Promises of Easter

Scripture: Matthew 28: 16-20

*I*t was about three o'clock that Friday afternoon when Jesus died on the cross. The observance of the Sabbath was to begin three hours later, so prompt action was called for and needed. According to the Jewish law of the day, a crucified victim could not remain on his cross over the Sabbath. Therefore, the body of Jesus had to be quickly taken down and quickly disposed of. (Those were harsh days back then.) And very often, the body of the crucified victim was simply thrown on the city garbage heap and left to be the prey of the circling vultures, the carrion crows, and the pariah dogs of the street.

But fortunately, the followers of Jesus had an influential friend who was able to help them pay what they thought (at that moment) was to be their last tribute to their fallen master. The friend was a powerful man named Joseph of Arimathea. He was rich and devout; a member of the Sanhedrin, and—in secret—he was a follower of Jesus. Joseph of Arimathea went to the Roman governor, Pontuis Pilate, and requested to be given the body of Jesus so that a decent burial could be performed. Pilate was surprised that Jesus had died so quickly, but he was willing to grant Joseph's request. So Joseph and Nicodemus (the man who had first visited Jesus by night) came and took the body and buried it in a cavelike tomb owned by Joseph. The grave was located in a garden very near the hill called Calvary. Then a great circular stone, shaped like the wheel of a cart and running in a groove, was rolled across the entrance to close up the tomb.

Meanwhile, the Temple authorities were still uneasy about Jesus. Even though they had seen him die on the cross, they were still nervous. The authorities went to Pilate and asked that special precautions be taken to guard the body, so that no one could steal it. Pilate agreed. He posted guards outside the tomb to guard it around the clock, and in addition he had the stone sealed to the entrance to make doubly sure that no one could get in—or out! Throughout Friday night, all day Saturday, and Saturday night, the body of Jesus lay in the tomb. There were no visitors coming to the grave, because it was the Sabbath, and that kind of travel or activity would have been a blatant violation of the Sabbath law.

But then came Sunday morning. Easter Sunday morning! Early that morning, while it was still dark, Mary Magdalene came to the tomb. She saw that the stone had been rolled away from the cave's entrance and that the grave was empty. Alarmed, Mary ran to fetch Simon Peter and John (see John 20:1-10). Together, they ran back to the grave site and found it just as Mary had described it—the stone pushed back and the tomb empty. Peter and John turned back toward home, trying to sort out what on earth this could mean, but Mary, so crestfallen, stayed there in the garden just outside the tomb to grieve and mourn alone. She wept softly. She thought someone had stolen Jesus' body. She wondered aloud: "How could they do this? Haven't they done enough? And now this. They have stolen his body! They have hidden it from us. Have they no shame? Have they no feelings at all?"

Then, in what some have called the greatest recognition scene in all of literature, Mary suddenly ran head-on into the Resurrection. She suddenly recognized the Risen Lord. At first she thought that he was the gardener, but when he called her name, "Mary," her eyes were opened to the truth of Easter. She saw with her own eyes the Risen Christ. And as always happens when we encounter the living Lord firsthand, he put her to work. He gave her a job. He sent her to tell the others the good news. So Mary ran as fast as her excited feet could carry her to find the other disciples, shouting, as she ran, the good news of Easter: "He is risen! He is risen! I have seen the Lord! Christ is risen!" (*Compare* with John 20.)

Isn't that a great story? If that story doesn't make you tingle all over with excitement, then you had better check your spiritual pulse. But you know, that's not the only story. The Gospels record numerous accounts of post-Resurrection appearances, all exciting, all amazing, all mind-boggling. For example, the risen Christ dramatically appeared to the disciples in the upper room, giving them the encouragement they needed; Jesus also appeared to Doubting Thomas, giving him the assurance he needed; he appeared to those two disillusioned men on the Emmaus Road, giving them the hope they needed; and he appeared to Simon Peter on the seashore, giving him the forgiveness he so desperately needed.

And in Matthew 28, we see yet another Resurrection appearance: The risen Christ appeared to his disciples on the mountaintop in Galilee, where he gave them the great commission to go and preach the gospel to all the people, "mak[ing] disciples of all nations, baptizing them in the name of the Father and of the Son and of the Holy Spirit" (verse 19). In this Scripture we see neatly outlined for us the very special gifts that Easter gives to us.

Do you give Easter gifts in your household? We do! I think for us, this practice dates back to childhood. When

I was a little boy, in addition to an Easter basket, I always received some new clothes and a new pair of shoes for Easter. In addition, we always bought beautiful spring corsages for my mother and grandmother, and we always took an Easter offering to the church. Do you remember those Easter offering folders with those little pouches that held a dime for each day of Lent? We would take those and lay them on the altar on Easter Sunday morning. Flowers, candy, clothes, Easter bonnets and Easter shoes, and Easter offerings: These were the gifts of Easter at our house.

It's a wonderful tradition, giving gifts to loved ones at Easter. But it's even better and much more important to receive the gifts that Easter has for us! Here they are in Matthew 28. We see in this Scripture that Easter gives us three gifts: (1) a Resurrection; (2) a mission; and (3) a promise.

First of All, Easter Gives Us a Resurrection

Easter gives us new life, new vitality, and a new sense of victory over sin, over despair, over defeat, and even over death.

One of the most dramatic stories ever to come from the sports world involved Lou Little, the famous football coach. One year he had a young man on his college football team who did not play very well or very often, but whose spirit boosted the morale of the entire team. His great attitude was an inspiration to everybody who knew him. Coach Little grew especially fond of the young man, and he admired the proud way the boy escorted his father arm in arm, around the campus whenever his father came to visit.

About a week before the season's biggest game, the boy's mother telephoned Coach Little to say that her husband had died that morning, and would he break the news to her son. When the young man returned to the campus after his father's funeral, he came in to see Coach Little and ask a very special favor. "I want to start the big game Saturday," he told the coach. "I think this is what my father would have liked most." Coach Little hesitated. He really felt that the young man was not good enough to play on the first string, but what could he do?

"Okay, son, I'll let you start, but I can only leave you in there for a couple of plays. This is the biggest game of the year." Coach Little kept his word and started the young man as he had promised. But he never took him out; the boy played sixty minutes of inspired football and led the team to victory! "What got into you?" Coach Little asked him after the game. The boy replied, "Do you remember how my father and I used to go around the campus arm in arm? There was something about him that very few people knew. He didn't want them to. My father was totally blind. This afternoon was the first time he ever saw me play!"

This is the good news of Easter, isn't it? The Resurrection. Christ conquered death, and through him—through faith in him and by his power and grace—so can we. It is interesting to note that on that first Easter, Christ was not the only one resurrected. The disciples were resurrected too! Look at them. After Good Friday, they were down and out, devastated and defeated, despondent and disillusioned. They were the very picture of death. But when they found the resurrected Christ, they found new life; no more trudging, no more weeping, no more complaining, no more self-pity. Now they were running, shouting, rejoicing, and celebrating. They had been reborn!

That's the first gift Easter gives to us—the gift of new life, rebirth, salvation; the gift of Resurrection.

Second, Easter Gives Us a Mission

With the good news of Resurrection came a new responsibility, a new calling, a new job, a new mission. The risen Christ—both then and now—sends his followers out into all the world with the message of his sacrificial love. "Go therefore and make disciples of all nations, baptizing them in the name of the Father and of the Son and of the Holy Spirit." Jesus encourages, "Take up the torch. Be my evangelists!"

Charles Schulz, the late creator of the "Peanuts" comic strip, was a devout Christian. He had an amazing perceptiveness as he viewed life, and often his faith experiences made their way into his comic strips. For example, there's the one where Lucy is talking to Linus about evangelism. She says, "You know, Linus, I would have made a good evangelist."

"What makes you think that?" responds Linus.

"Well," Lucy says, "do you know that kid who sits behind me at school? I convinced him that my religion is better than his religion."

"How did you do that?" Linus asks.

Lucy replies, "I hit him with my lunch box!"

Well, we get the point that Charles Schulz was making. Some people are like Lucy. They come on strong. They are heavy-handed in their evangelism techniques. Charles Schulz, over the years, had probably been hit a time or two with some religious "lunch boxes"! It is true that throughout church history and right up to the present day, some religious people have indeed tried to evangelize others with coercion and intimidation, with fear and force, with guilt and shame, with threats and even violence.

But that is not the spirit of Christ. That is not the way Christ chose. He turned away from those kinds of tactics

68

when he was tempted in the wilderness, and he chose instead the way of sacrificial love, a self-giving love that went to and through the cross. On the cross, Jesus Christ made it clear that the message is love and grace, that he wants us not to force people into faith, but to *love* them into it. He wants us to share the lunch with them, not hit them with our lunch box! Let me show you what I mean.

A minister friend tells about a troubled young woman who came to his church a few years ago. She was very depressed. Her life was full of pain and disappointment, and she was on the brink of suicide that Sunday morning when she walked into the sanctuary. As the congregation members sang and shared the joy of their faith, she began to feel even worse because she felt that she had nothing to sing about or rejoice over.

But when the service ended, a very beautiful and special thing happened. An older woman in the church, who was severely disabled with arthritis and could hardly move, made her way, with some effort, down the pew to simply greet this troubled woman and welcome her to church. When this beautiful, welcoming gesture occurred, it was more than the troubled young woman could handle, and she broke down and began to cry. The older woman cradled the young woman in her arms and let her weep. She held her and gently rocked her, and she let her cry.

Then they talked a little and prayed together, just the two of them, all alone now in the sanctuary. The older woman invited the young woman to come home with her for lunch, and the invitation was accepted. That simple gesture of love opened up a brand-new life and a brand-new beginning for this troubled woman. And some months later, she wrote a note to her new friend, the older woman, and the young woman said this to her: "I cannot think of you for five minutes without thinking of God! In your love I have found a place in His love, and through the Christ I have seen in you, I have now discovered the Christ in me too!"

For sure, Easter gives us a Resurrection, but Easter also gives us that important mission to take God's sacrificial love to a troubled and hurting world.

Finally, Along with a Resurrection and a Mission, Easter Gives Us a Promise

Easter gives us the promise of God's strong presence always with us, the promise that God will never desert us. Remember how Jesus put it: "I am with you always, to the end of the age" (Matthew 28:20).

No matter what problems or persecutions we have to face, no matter what obstacles or adversaries we encounter, there is one thing we can always count on: the promise of God to always be with us. Nothing, not even death, can separate us from God and God's love through Christ Jesus.

I recently heard a story about a father and his young daughter who were on a cruise together. It was a "getaway" cruise for them, because the man's wife—the little girl's mother—had just died, and they were trying to do something special to help relieve the pain. There on the deck of the ship one morning, the little girl asked her father a really tough question. "Daddy," she said, "does God love us as much as Mommy did?" The father was taken aback by the question at first. He didn't know what to say. This was an important question, and he knew he couldn't sidestep it. Finally, he pointed out across the water to the distant horizon. "Honey," he said, "God's love reaches farther than you can see in that direction." And then he turned around and said, "And

God's love reaches farther than you can see in that direction too." Then the young father looked up at the sky and said, "And God's love is higher than the sky." And then he pointed down at the ocean and said, "And it's deeper than the ocean as well."

The little girl said a beautiful thing. She said, "Just think, Daddy, we're right here in the big middle of it all!"

That says it all, doesn't it? We live in the "big middle" of God's strong presence and watchful care, with a Resurrection, a mission, and a promise: with a resurrection of life, a mission of love, and a promise that we can count on. Don't miss that.

Don't miss the great promises of Easter.

❧ 7 ❧
Don't Miss . . .
The Rest of the Story

Scripture: John 21:15-19

Many of you are familiar with the noted radio broadcast personality Paul Harvey and his nationally syndicated program called "The Rest of the Story." It has a fascinating format. Paul Harvey will tell a colorful human-interest story that sometimes seems to be heading toward a bleak, negative, or even disastrous conclusion. Then, just when you are expecting the worst, just when you are all set up to hear a sad and dismal ending, Paul Harvey will go to a commercial break with these words: "When we come back, I'll tell you the *rest* of the story."

Now, "the *rest* of the story," of course, always provides the inevitable surprise ending—frequently an amazing conclusion about courage or heroism or perseverance or redemption or love or reconciliation. I don't know if Paul Harvey and his staff have ever thought of this, but Easter is the perfect example of this "The Rest of the Story" idea. On Maundy Thursday evening when Jesus was arrested, things looked pretty bleak. And then on Good Friday when he was savagely nailed to that cross, it looked like a disastrous ending. But then came Easter Sunday morning—and "the *rest* of the story"!

Christ had conquered death.

Christ had defeated the grave.

Christ had risen.

Christ had won the victory.

End of story? Well, not quite, because in John 21:15-19 we have what we might call "the *rest* of the rest of the story"! In other words, after the Resurrection, *then* what? This is precisely what this poignant passage in John 21 is all about, especially when we see it through the eyes of Simon Peter. Remember the story with me. Simon Peter and his friends had been waiting there in Galilee for some time—just waiting—waiting for some direction from God, but nothing had happened. No word. *Where* is *the risen Lord, anyway? Why doesn't he come on, and tell us what we are supposed to do now?*

Finally, in typical fashion, Simon Peter got impatient. He couldn't take it anymore. He had these deep guilt feelings rumbling around in his soul, because he felt so ashamed that he—Peter "the Rock"—had crumbled under the pressure, and in "crunch time" had denied his Lord, not once, but three times. And now, all this waiting was only making him agonize over that all the more. It was driving him up the wall. And suddenly, with a tone of agitation, he said, "I'm going fishing!" Now, what Simon Peter meant is this: "I can't handle this any longer. This waiting around is eating me up. I'm worn out with the indecision, the waiting around, the risks involved. I don't know about the rest of you, but I am *out* of here. I'm going fishing. I'm going back to the old, secure life, the old life of being a fisherman."

The others were used to following Simon's lead, so they went along with him. They fished all night, but with no luck. But then, as dawn broke, they saw someone standing on the shore. It was Jesus, the risen Lord, but they didn't recognize him at this point. Jesus told them to cast their nets on the right side of the boat. They did so and brought in a huge catch of fish—153 large fish. The lightbulb came on for John, and he turned and said to Peter, "It is the Lord!" Simon Peter, always excitable and impulsive, dove in and urgently swam to shore. The others came in on the boat. As they came ashore, they saw the risen Christ cooking breakfast for them over a charcoal fire.

After Christ served the disciples breakfast (another Holy Communion), he took Simon Peter off to the side; and as we read this in the Scriptures, we experience one of the most beautiful and moving moments in all of Scripture. Three times Christ asked Simon Peter the same question: "Simon, do you love me?"

"Oh, yes, Lord," Simon Peter answered, "You know I love you."

"Then feed my sheep," the risen Lord said to him. Of course, it's obvious what's going on here in the Scriptures. Christ is forgiving Simon Peter and is giving him the chance to profess his faith and love three times, an opportunity for Simon Peter to make up for his earlier threefold denial.

Now, don't miss this. The story ends exactly the way it started months before, with Christ saying to Simon Peter at the seashore these powerful words: "Follow me" (see Matthew 4:18-19). Look at this. The first thing and the last thing Jesus said to Simon Peter was that simple command: "Follow me!" We know the rest of the story. Simon Peter went on to become the bold and courageous leader of the early church. Boldly, he gave his life to Christ, and courageously he gave his life for the church. You know why that happened, don't you? Because that day long ago on the seashore, the risen Lord came looking for Simon Peter to give him his love, to give him his forgiveness, and to give him his ministry.

And those are the same three things that Jesus Christ wants to give to you and to me right now, at this moment! Let me show you what I mean.

First of All, Jesus Christ Wants to Give Us His Love

The risen Christ came looking for Simon Peter that morning to give him his love, to love him back into the circle, to love him back into leadership. My friend Mark Trotter tells a story about a time when he flew to Nashville to attend a meeting there. He got to the airport late, about 10 P.M. He got his bags and went out to the curb to wait for the shuttle buses that take you to the hotels. There were a few other people standing there lined along the curb, wrapped in overcoats, trying to keep warm.

At the far end of the line sat a woman and her male companion, perched upon their own luggage. The man was silent; she was not. She was talking to her companion a mile a minute, and to anybody else within the sound of her voice—which, due to the volume level of her speaking voice, could have been the entire population of the county. She turned to the man standing next to her and said, "Where are you from?" He told her. She then began to tell him all about his city. Next, she turned to someone further down the line. "Where are *you* from?" The man told her, and she proceeded to tell him everything she knew about his city. She was working her way down the line, interrogating everybody standing along the curb, all the while sitting on her luggage, smoking one cigarette after another, complaining about how cold it was, and announcing that she could hardly wait to get to the hotel so she could go to the bar and have a drink.

"Where are you from?" she said loudly to the next person in line. Now, Mark Trotter is a somewhat shy person, and as she was getting closer to him, he started inching his way down the curb, trying to get as far away from her as he could. Just then, a hotel shuttle drove up. Everybody on the curb boarded that bus, except for the man, the woman, and Mark. Mark said he was certain that everyone who got on the van was not going to that hotel! He said it was like one of those showdown scenes in a western movie, where Main Street clears and there's nobody left but the sheriff on one end of the street and the outlaw at the other end.

"What hotel are you going to?" she asked. Mark told her. "Hey, *we're* going there too." Mark didn't say anything. She said, "I bet you're a lawyer."

"No," Mark said, "I just like to dress this way."

"Well, what do you *do*?"

"I'm a preacher," said Mark.

The woman replied, "Oh, my Lord!"

Mark said, "No Ma'am, I just work for him."

The shuttle arrived. They got in; along with the driver, there were just the three of them in the van. And in that van, Mark learned "the rest of the story." The woman said, "Preacher, I want you to meet my friend." She introduced Mark to her companion.

Mark said, "Hello, nice to meet you," and shook the man's hand. The man didn't respond.

So the woman said, "He don't talk. Cancer got his voice box. But I *love* this man. He's my friend. I love this man more than anything else in all the world!" Turning back to Mark, she said, "The doctor says he doesn't have long to live. We've come down here to Nashville to go to the Grand Ole Opry. I've got us tickets for tomorrow night. He said he always wanted to go to the Opry, and I'm going to take him. The next day I'm going to rent a car. We're going to drive down to Memphis. We're going to Graceland. He always wanted to go there too. Then we're going home. Oh, we're going to have a great time, aren't we?" she said as she hugged her friend tightly.

"We're going to have an absolutely wonderful time. Now, Preacher, you pray for him, you hear? Might do him some good. *Promise* me, now, you'll pray for him."

Now, obviously, there are lots of things in that woman's life that need work, but you can't help but admire that kind of self-giving, sacrificial love and compassion. When you see the love in that woman, you suddenly see her in a totally different light. Still rough around the edges, but the love shines through.

Some years ago, a young missionary went to succeed an older missionary who was retiring. The younger man said to the older veteran, "What are the three most important things you can tell me about this mission station?"

The older missionary said, "Love the people; love the people; love the people." That's the first thing we learn from this great passage in John 21. The risen Christ came looking for Simon Peter to give him the encouraging love he so desperately needed, and to remind him to pass that love on to the rest of the flock. "If you love me, then love my sheep," Jesus said.

First, Jesus Christ wants to give us his love.

Second, He Wants to Give Us His Forgiveness

Sam Houston, the American general and politician who became the president of Texas prior to its statehood, joined the church at the age of sixty. He wrote to a friend: "They told me that being baptized would wash away all my sins. If that be the case, I pity those poor souls living downstream." That's sort of the way Simon Peter felt that day. He felt ashamed and inadequate. He felt as though he had talked a good game and then "wimped out": "I denied my Lord three times. *Three times*! Count 'em! What if I do that again? Maybe I'm just a coward at heart. Maybe I should just go back to the old, safe life on my fishing boat. How could he ever forgive me anyway? How could he ever trust me again? I bragged, I boasted about my strength and commitment, I talked big—but then when the crisis came, I let him down. I let him down."

That's what Simon Peter was feeling that day, and that's why he was so quick to jump into the water (a new baptism perhaps?) and rush to the shore. Simon Peter had always been impetuous, but this was something more. It was Peter's way of saying, "I'm so sorry I failed you, Lord. I want to be the first to shore, the first in your presence, because I am so sorry that I failed you." Jesus was very perceptive. He knew what was going on deep down inside of Simon Peter, and just as he had given Doubting Thomas the reassurance and encouragement that he had needed (letting Thomas physically touch his scars), Jesus was now reaching out to touch Simon Peter emotionally and spiritually with the help and healing that he needed so desperately. Jesus took Simon Peter aside and forgave him, and in effect Jesus said to him, "Simon, I still believe in you. You are still 'the Rock.' You can do it, but you have to put your failure behind you. You are forgiven. The slate is wiped clean. You can start over again!"

I recently ran across a poem that caught my attention. It's called "The Land of Beginning Again," by Louisa Fletcher Tarkington, and it goes like this.

I wish there were some wonderful place,
In the Land of Beginning Again:
Where all our mistakes and all our heartaches
And all our poor selfish grief
Could be dropped like a shabby old coat at the door
And never be put on again.

Well, it just so happens that there *is* such a place. Simon Peter found that place on the seashore that morning. He found there the good news of the Christian faith. We can be forgiven. We can make a new beginning. This is precisely what the risen Christ does for us. He knows about our failures and our sins and our fears, and he comes looking for us to give us the love and the forgiveness that we so desperately need.

Third and Finally, He Wants to Give Us His Ministry

In this breakfast-at-the-sea passage in John 21, we have one of the most remarkable scenes found anywhere in the Bible. Throughout the New Testament, Jesus has been referred to as a king, a shepherd, a teacher, and a healer. Here in John 21, we see him as a cook, standing by a charcoal fire, ready to serve breakfast to his disciples. The reason for the breakfast meeting was specific. Jesus knew that his earthly ministry was over. If his ministry was to continue, someone had to pick up his cross; someone had to take up his torch; someone had to give strong leadership; someone had to rise to the occasion.

So the risen Lord came to Simon Peter and said, "If you love me, feed my sheep." And he is saying the same thing to you and me right now! The point is this: The best way to love Christ is to take up his ministry. He doesn't want burnt offerings or animal sacrifices or long, flowery, verbose prayers, or painfully pious expressions. He just wants us to take up his ministry of love.

Recently, I ran across an article that impressed me. The article shows how a ministry is different from a job. It says:

If you're doing it just well enough to get by, it's a job.
If you're doing it to the best of your ability, it's a ministry.
If you'll do it only so long as it doesn't interfere with other activities, it's a job.
If you're committed to staying with it, even when it means letting go of other things, it's a ministry.
If you quit because no one praised you or thanked you, it was a job.
If you stay with it even when no one seems to notice, it's a ministry.
If you do it because someone else said it needs to be done, it's a job.
If you do it because you are convinced it needs to be done, it's a ministry.
It's hard to get excited about a job.
It's impossible not to get excited about a ministry.
People may say "well done" when you do your job.
The Lord will say "well done" when you complete your ministry.

(*Indian River United Methodist Church Newsletter,* January 1998)

That's what I love so much about the breakfast-by-the-sea passage in John 21. It powerfully shows us how the risen Christ comes to Simon Peter and to us to give us something we had better not miss: his love, his forgiveness, and his ministry.

✿ 8 ✿

Don't Miss . . .

God's Surprises

Scripture: Acts: 2:1-4

D o you remember the old story about the two men who were having lunch together one day? One man said to the other, "Let me ask you something. Do you realize how lucky you are to have your wife? She is so outstanding in every way. Bright, articulate, radiant, personable, kind, and thoughtful—a great mother, beautiful inside and out; she has a successful career, and she is so devoted to you! She is a terrific person, and I just wondered if you realize how fortunate you are, and whether you ever tell her how much you love her and appreciate her."

"Well, I do realize how great she is," the husband said, "but the truth is I probably do take her for granted. The truth is, I haven't expressed my love for her as I should. But this conversation has inspired me, and I'm going to do better, I promise you that!"

The husband decided to "get with the program" immediately. That very night, he would give his wife "a night to remember" as a symbol of his love. He went down to the leading department store and bought the dress that she had been admiring in the showcase window. While he was there, he bought her a large bottle of her favorite perfume. Then he ordered tickets for the evening performance of the Broadway play she had been hoping to see. He made reservations at her favorite restaurant. And he ordered two dozen long-stemmed red roses for her.

When he arrived home that night, he exploded through the door, hugged his wife affectionately, and told her what he had done. He told her about the restaurant and the play. He gave her the dress, the perfume, and the flowers. And then he said in his most romantic voice: "I've done all this for you, my darling, for no other reason than to simply say dramatically tonight what I feel in my heart all the time—that I love you, I adore you, I appreciate you!"

Immediately, his wife burst into tears. "What is this?" he said. "Why are you crying? I thought these expressions of love would make you happy."

To this, his wife replied, "This has been the worst day of my life! It was just awful at the office. We lost our biggest account, my coworkers were obnoxious, and my clients were totally unreasonable. On top of that, things have been even worse here at the house. The children have been absolutely terrible. They have torn up the house and they broke my favorite lamp, the maid got mad and quit, the water heater burst, the washing machine broke down again, and now, to top it all off, surprise of surprises: You have come home drunk!"

Like that well-intentioned, slow-to-come-around husband, when we start doing good things for other people, we may indeed surprise some folks. But we ought to do those gracious, loving acts anyway.

Something like that occurred on the Day of Pentecost. Something quite wonderful happened there, and some tried to dismiss it with a wave of the hand, saying, "Oh, don't pay any attention to those Jesus followers! They are just drunk; too much new wine! Think nothing of it. Just ignore them!"

But those followers of Jesus were not drunk, and they would not be ignored. They were filled all right, but not with new wine. They were filled with new power, new spark, new courage, new enthusiasm, new hope, new confidence, because they were filled with the Holy Spirit of God!

Remember the story with me. The followers of Jesus were gathered together in one place. Earlier, they had experienced together the agony of Good Friday. They had seen their Lord brutally crucified. But then they had experienced together the ecstasy of Easter. They had seen the risen Lord, and they too had become resurrected in the faith! Then together they had watched the Lord leave the earth, ascending into heaven to be with God the Father.

Now, here's where the story of Pentecost picks up. The disciples were gathered and waiting. Suddenly, a sound came from heaven; like the rush of a mighty wind, the breath of God filled that place. The Spirit of God touched them, and suddenly they began to rejoice and speak and celebrate and communicate. This is the moment they had been waiting for, and now, here it was!

A crowd gathered to see what in the world was going on, and an amazing thing happened. People were there from most everywhere, from most every nation, and each one heard these followers of Jesus describing the mighty works of God. And here is what's incredible: Each person in that crowd—regardless of his or her country of origin and native language—heard the message of Jesus' followers in his or her own native language! "This is astounding! What can this mean?" someone said out loud. "Aw, they're just drunk!" somebody else shouted.

That was all the prompting Simon Peter needed. He stood tall and he addressed the entire gathering: "These are not drunk people," he said to them. "These are people filled with the Spirit of God, and they are speaking the truth of God. Jesus of Nazareth was God's Word to us, but you wouldn't listen! You crucified him. You tried to silence him, but you can't kill God's Truth! It resurrects! God raised him up!"

When the people heard Peter's words, they were cut to the heart. They were ashamed, and they were afraid. But Peter said to them, "What you did to the Son of God was a terrible thing, but even still, it is not too late for you. You can be forgiven! And you too can receive God's Spirit." The story ends by telling us that on that Day of Pentecost, some three thousand people repented and believed and were baptized (*see* Acts 2:41).

We see here in the story of Pentecost one of the great threads that runs throughout the Bible, namely, the element of surprise! All through the Scriptures, we see God surprising people: appearing in a burning bush, rolling back the waters of the Red Sea, coming to visit the earth in the form of a little baby, and (surprise of surprises!) using, of all things, a cross—a tool of torture and death—as the instrument of salvation.

And here at Pentecost, jumping dramatically out of this story we see three of God's most wonderful, amazing surprises. Here they are.

First of All, We See at Pentecost God's Surprising Love for All People

All of the people heard the message of God that day. Real love is inclusive! It is goodwill toward all people. Real love sees all people as children of God. Sometimes we have trouble with that, don't we? Every day we see it in our newspapers—more stories of violence. We want to pick and choose who to love and who to be nice to. But this wasn't a problem at Pentecost, was it? What happened there was open and available to all the people, and God's message was spread in a language that each person could understand.

Do you recall the "Calvin & Hobbes" comic strip? It was really quite wonderful. Bill Watterson cleverly created this cartoon strip about a little six-year-old boy named Calvin and his toy tiger named Hobbes. When adults were around, Hobbes the tiger was a small, stuffed animal, but when Calvin and Hobbes were alone, Hobbes became a tall, life-size, imaginary friend.

In one of the strips, Calvin and Hobbes accidentally push the family car down the driveway, losing control of it. It gets away from them and rolls down into the street. Knowing that they are in big trouble, Calvin and Hobbes go into a panic. They run away and hide in a neighbor's tree.

Calvin's mother spots them up in the tree. "There you are, Calvin! Come down so I can talk to you!"

"No!" cries Calvin. "You'll spank us for what we did. We're running away from home!"

"I'm not going to spank you," his mother reassures him. "I just want to find out what happened and be sure you're all right. Are you okay? Was anyone hurt?"

"No," Calvin replies. "No one was hurt. We were pushing the car into the drive and it kept rolling."

"The car didn't hit anything?" his mother asks.

"No. It just went across the road and into the ditch. And that's when we took off."

"Well," said his mother, "I called the tow truck and they pulled it out, and there's no damage." Then, holding out her arms to him, Calvin's mother says, "So, Calvin, you can come down and come home now."

Calvin peeks his head around the tree trunk and says to his mother, "I'll come down and I'll come home—but first let's hear you say you love me!"

Calvin was pretty smart. He knew that forgiveness begins and ends in love. This is the message of Pentecost. God comes in the person of the Holy Spirit to love and forgive, and this love is offered to all people everywhere.

But, as Peter put it, we have to repent and believe and accept God's love in faith.

Recently I had a picture taken. "I hope you will do me justice," I said to the photographer. With a grin, the photographer replied, "What you need is not justice, but mercy!" Don't we all need mercy? The surprising good news of God is that God is indeed merciful to all of us, and God wants to include all of us in the circle of his love. He loves each one of us! And what's more, God wants us to love one another.

God's love for all people; that's the number one surprise from God at Pentecost. Now, here is a second surprise.

Second, We See at Pentecost God's Surprising Presence in Unexpected Places

Have you ever met God in an unexpected place? Some of the most memorable moments in the Scriptures are those accounts of people running up on God in unexpected places. For example:

- Moses, in exile in the wilderness, finds God there in a burning bush.
- Jacob, in the most fearful moment of his life—wrestling with his soul—finds God there.
- Elijah, wallowing in self-pity, thinking suicidal thoughts, finds God there.
- Job finds God in the midst of tragedy, suffering, and pain.
- Shadrach, Meshach, and Abednego find God in a fiery furnace.
- Daniel finds God in the lion's den.

And whoever would have thought that God's spirit would explode dramatically into the world through that little, motley handful of disciples at Pentecost!

Surprisingly, sometimes when we least expect it, suddenly God is there with power and grace.

Some of you will recognize the name of Clarence Jordan. He died in 1969 after a lifetime of sharing the gospel with others. He will probably be remembered most for his homespun translation of the Scriptures, which he titled *The Cottonpatch Version*. When Clarence Jordan died, many of his friends reminisced about the vibrant qualities of his life—his strength and gentleness, his commitment and sense of humor, his simple life and eloquent words, and his ability to be at ease with people from all walks of life.

Clarence Jordan was buried on a hillside that is part of Koinonia Farms, the bold faith community that he and his wife had founded. At his funeral, a beautiful thing happened. People were sobbing, moaning, and grieving as men shoveled the soil of Georgia on top of his cedar casket. But just then a little two-year-old girl, who lived on the farm, unprompted and spontaneously stepped up to the grave and sang her favorite song. She had sensed that this was a special day for her friend Clarence. So, boldly in her little two year old voice, she sang this song for him: "Happy birthday to you, happy birthday to you. Happy birthday, Dear Clarence, happy birthday to you."

"A little child shall lead them"; so say the Scriptures (Isaiah 11:6). And that day in Georgia, a little two-year-old child led those grieving people into the presence of God. With her simple song, she reminded them that death is not death at all for the Christian. No; it's a *birth* day! Those people at that funeral had found God before in expected places—in church, in prayer, in the Scriptures, at the altar. But suddenly God was with them as never before in the unexpected place of grief and sorrow.

Isn't it something? God's surprising love for all people, and God's surprising presence in unexpected places.

Finally, We See at Pentecost God's Surprising Judgment of What We Fail to Do

It wasn't just that they crucified Jesus. It was also that they failed to listen to him, they failed to follow him, they failed to stand tall with him. It's not just what we *do*; we are also accountable to God for what we *fail* to do. Think of it: the elder brother, the one-talent servant, the priest and the Levite, the foolish maiden, Pontius Pilate—all depict graphically the sin of *omission*, the sin of failing to do what we ought to do.

There is an old Japanese legend that makes the point dramatically. It tells of a man who died and went to heaven. As he was shown around, he was much impressed with the sights—beautiful gardens where lotus flowers bloomed, mansions built of marble and gold and precious stones. It was all so beautiful, even more wonderful than he had imagined!

But then the man came to a very large room that looked like a merchant's shop. Lining the walls were shelves on which were piled and labeled what looked very much like dried mushrooms. On closer examination, however, the newcomer to heaven saw that they were not mushrooms at all. Actually, they were human ears! His guide explained that these were the ears of people on earth who went diligently to their places of worship and listened with pleasure to the teachings of faith, yet did nothing about what they heard; so after death, they, themselves, went somewhere else, and only their ears reached heaven!

What a surprising God! He surprisingly loves all people with tender mercy. He surprisingly shows up in the most unexpected places. He surprisingly holds us accountable for the things we fail to do. Now, that's something to think about, isn't it?

❧ 9 ❧

Don't Miss . . .
The Chance for a Second Birth

Scripture: John 3:1-16

His name was Paul. He lived in a small town in the Pacific Northwest some years ago. He was just a little boy when his family became the proud owners of one of the first telephones in the neighborhood. It was one of those wooden boxes attached to the wall, with the shiny receiver hanging on the side of the box and the mouthpiece attached to the front.

Young Paul listened with fascination as his mother and father used the phone, and he discovered that somewhere inside the wonderful device called a telephone lived an amazing person. Her name was "Information Please," and there was nothing she did not know. Information Please could supply anybody's number, as well as the correct time! Paul's first personal experience with "Information Please" came one day when he was home alone and he whacked his finger with a hammer. The pain was terrible, and he didn't know what to do. And then Paul thought of the telephone. Quickly, he pulled a footstool up to the phone, climbed up, unhooked the receiver, held it to his ear, and said, "Information Please" into the mouthpiece.

There was a click or two, and then a small, clear voice spoke: "Information."

"I hurt my finger!" Paul wailed into the phone.

"Isn't your mother home?"

"Nobody's home but me!" Paul cried.

"Are you bleeding?"

"No," Paul said. "I hit my finger with the hammer, and it hurts."

"Can you open your icebox?"

"Yes."

"Then go get some ice and hold it to your finger." Paul did this, and it helped a lot.

After that, Paul called "Information Please" for everything. She helped him with his geography and his math. She taught him how to spell the word *fix*. She told him what to feed his pet chipmunk. And then when Paul's pet canary died, she tenderly listened to his grieving and said, "Paul, always remember that there are other worlds to sing in." Somehow that helped, and Paul felt better.

When Paul was nine years old, he moved with his family to Boston, and as the years passed, he missed "Information Please" very much. Some years later, as Paul was on his way out west to go to college, his plane landed in Seattle. He dialed his hometown operator and said, "Information Please." Miraculously, he heard that same small, clear voice that he knew so well: "Information." Paul hadn't planned this, but suddenly he blurted out, "Could you please tell me how to spell the word *fix*?"

There was a long pause. Then came the soft answer: "I guess your finger must be all healed by now!"

Paul laughed. "So it's really still *you*! Do you have any idea how much you meant to me during that time when I was a little boy?"

"I wonder," she said, "if you know how much your calls meant to me! I never had any children, and I used to look forward to your calls so much."

Paul told her how much he had missed her over the

years and asked if he could call her again when he was back in the area. "Please do," she said. "Just ask for Sally." Three months later, Paul was back in Seattle. This time, a different voice answered. Paul asked for Sally.

"Are you a friend?" the operator asked.

"Yes, a very old friend." Paul answered.

"Well, I'm sorry to have to tell you this," she said. "Sally had been working part time the last few years because she was sick. She died five weeks ago." Before Paul could hang up, the operator said, "Wait a minute. Did you say your name was Paul?"

"Yes," Paul replied.

"Well, Sally left a message for you. She wrote it down in case you called. Let me read it to you. It says: 'When Paul calls, tell him that I still say: There are other worlds to sing in.' He will know what I mean." Paul thanked her and hung up, and he *did* know what Sally meant.

"There are other worlds to sing in." Isn't that a beautiful and powerful thought? And this is precisely what the message in John 3 is all about. "There are other worlds to sing in"—in this life, and, yes, even beyond this life. When Jesus said to Nicodemus that night, "You must be born again. You must be born from above," that's what he meant: You don't have to stay the way you are; you can make a new start. You can have a new life. You can become a new person. There are other worlds to sing in.

Remember the story with me.

Nicodemus was a key leader among the Jews in the time of Jesus. He was probably from a wealthy, distinguished, and highly respected family. He was a Pharisee, one of a brotherhood of six thousand who had taken a pledge in front of three witnesses that they would dedicate their lives to observing every detail of the scribal law. The scribes worked out the regulations. The Pharisees consecrated their lives to keeping them to the nth degree. In addition, Nicodemus was a member of the Sanhedrin, the Supreme Court of the Jews. The Sanhedrin had only seventy-one members out of the six thousand Pharisees. These top seventy-one made up the Sandhedrin jury, and Nicodemus was one of them. The Sanhedrin had religious authority over every Jew in the world, and one of its primary duties was to examine and deal with anyone suspected of being a false prophet.

Nicodemus came to visit Jesus by night, and much has been written about this. Why did Nicodemus come by night? Was he afraid of "guilt by association"? Was he fearful of what his Pharisee colleagues might think? Or did he want a private audience with Jesus, undisturbed? Was he coming as a "watchdog" of the Sanhedrin? Or was he genuinely interested in getting to know Jesus better? All of these are fascinating questions, but what is amazing here is that he came to Jesus at all. Nicodemus's Pharisee friends would have scoffed at this thought. After all, Jesus was not one of them, and besides, they were supremely suspicious of him. The Pharisees had identified him as a troublemaker who was upsetting the people, and they were looking for an opportunity to silence him. They saw Jesus as a threat.

But Nicodemus came to Jesus and said to him, "Rabbi, you must be a teacher who has come from God because no one could do the signs and wonders you do apart from the presence of God." And Jesus responded to Nicodemus by saying to him, "You can't see the kingdom of God without being born again. You must be born from above." Jesus was saying that you can't become a Christian by making a few minor adjustments to your life. It must be a complete turnaround, a radical rebirth, a rebirth from above, which, of course, means a new life from God. Nicodemus didn't understand. He didn't get it. So, Jesus explained with what many would call the greatest verse in all of the Bible, John 3:16: "For God so loved the world that he gave his only Son, so that everyone who believes in him may not perish but may have eternal life."

Some years ago, the great boxer Muhammad Ali was asked by an urban youth how he, the youth, could quit school and start a boxing career, since he had bad grades. Ali smiled at the young man and said in his poetic fashion:

Stay in college and get the knowledge,
And stay there 'til you're through;
If [God] can make penicillin out of moldy bread,
[God] can make something out of you!

This is the good news of John 3. Because God so loved the world, he sent his only Son to make something out of us. When we accept him into our lives and commit our hearts to him, then he gives us new life in this world and new life in the world to come. This is what it means to be "born again" or "born from above." But let me be more specific and describe this new birth with three thoughts. You will think of other dimensions of this rebirth through Christ, but for now, let's try these three on for size.

First of All, to Be Born from Above Means to Come Alive to the Bible

In his book *Biblical Proclamation for Africa Today* ([Nashville: Abingdon Press, 1995], pp. 15-16), John Wesley Zwomunondiita Kurewa tells a wonderful story about a young woman who had heard people talking about an interesting new book that had just been published. Everybody raved about how great it was. She went to the bookstore, found a copy, bought it, took it home, and tried to read it, but somehow she just couldn't get interested in it. She would read a little and then put the book aside. It did not capture her attention.

A few months later, the young woman was traveling in a foreign country. She met a handsome young man, and she fell in love with him. As they spent time together, she discovered that he was a writer. And would you believe it? He was the author of that book everyone was talking about back home, the one she had bought and tried to read, but it failed to hold her attention. When the woman returned home, she found the book and started reading it again, and this time, she couldn't put it down! She read it from cover to cover, and then she read it again and again. It was the most exciting, most wonderful book she had ever read in her life! What was the difference? Simply this: She now had met the author. She knew him personally. He was her friend; indeed, she was in love with him.

This story is a wonderful parable for what it means to "come alive" to the Bible. If we don't know Christ personally, the Bible is hard to read, difficult to get into, easy to put aside. But when we know Christ personally and intimately, when we feel his love and *return* his love, then the Bible comes alive for us. It becomes a "love letter" from God; it becomes the most exciting book we have ever read in our life!

There is a fascinating thing to notice about Nicodemus in John 3. He knew his Scriptures well. But for him, being religious meant knowing what to do and especially what *not* to do. The emphasis of his Bible study was on what people do. But Jesus changed all of that. Jesus said that in order to see the kingdom of God, the emphasis must shift to what *God* does. The New

Testament makes it clear that this "new birth" is not our doing. We are "born from above." This is God's gift. We can't earn it; we can only accept it in faith. So to be "born from above" means to come alive to the Bible by falling in love with "the author and finisher of our faith."

Second, to Be Born from Above Means to Come Alive to Love

When our granddaughter, Sarah, was six years old, she went to the doctor for a checkup. As the doctor came into the examining room, Sarah held up both hands to get his attention, and then she said, "Dr. Ames, I know what you are going to do. You are going to do five things. You are going to check my eyes, my ears, my nose, my throat, and my heart."

Dr. Ames smiled and said, "Well, Sarah, that is exactly right. Is there any particular order I should go in?"

Sarah said, "You can go in any order you want to, but if I were you, I'd start with the heart!" That's what Jesus did, isn't it? He started with the heart. He started with love, and that is precisely what he wants us to do!

Nicodemus and his Pharisee friends had a hard time with that because they had been taught all of their lives to start with all those laws and rules and regulations and restrictions. For example, if a man fell into a hole on the Sabbath day and was screaming for help, the Pharisee would say, "What does the law say about this? Let's see, the law says, 'You can't work on the Sabbath day,'" so the Pharisee's response to the man in distress would be, "Sorry, I can't help you today. Maybe somebody will come along tomorrow. Sorry, you know that I can't break the scribal law." On the other hand, Jesus would start with the heart, and he would say to the man in the hole, "Give me your hand. I'll pull you out!"

That night in Jerusalem long ago, Jesus was saying to Nicodemus—and to us—"You don't have to stay the way you are. You don't have to be a prisoner to legalism. There are other worlds to sing in. You can be reborn from above. You can come alive to the Bible, and you can come alive to love!"

Third and Finally, to Be Born from Above Means to Come Alive to Eternal Life

For the Christian, death is not death at all. It is not the end of life. It is simply moving through a door called "death" into a new dimension of life with God.

Some years ago, I received a letter from a good friend. His mother had died, and after her funeral someone had sent him a copy of Henry Van Dyke's "Parable of Immortality." The words meant a lot to my friend, and he shared them with me. The message is very powerful. Henry Van Dyke, reflecting on the meaning of death and eternal life with God, wrote:

> I am standing on the seashore. A ship at my side spreads her white sails to the morning breeze and starts for the blue ocean. She is an object of beauty and strength, and I stand and watch until at last she hangs like a speck of white cloud just where the sea and sky come down to mingle with each other. Then someone at my side says, "There she goes!"
>
> "Gone where?" Gone from my sight—that is all. She is just as large in mast and hull and span as she was when she left my sight and just as able to bear her load of living freight to the place of her destination. Her diminished size is in me, not in her. And just at the moment when someone at my side says, "There she goes!" there are other eyes—watching her coming and other voices ready to take up the glad shout, "Here she comes! Here she comes!" on the other shore.

This is the good news of our Christian faith. We can be born again in this life, and we can be born yet again when death comes, because there are other worlds to sing in. When we commit our lives to Christ, God will always be there for us, even on the other side of the grave. We can count on that, because we know that "God so loved the world that he gave his only Son, so that everyone who believes in him may not perish but may have eternal life."

Being "born from above" means many things, but for sure it means accepting Jesus Christ into our lives as our personal Savior—and through him, coming alive to the Bible, coming alive to Christlike love, and coming alive to eternal life. Please don't miss that!

❧ 10 ❧

Don't Miss . . .
The Leap of Faith

Scripture: 2 Kings 5:1-14

*L*et me share with you some fascinating quotations. See if you can find the common thread that runs through them and links them together:

- In the 1920s, David Sarnoff was trying to convince his business associates to invest in radio. They said, "The wireless music box has no imaginable commercial value. Who on earth would pay for a message sent to nobody in particular?"

- In 1876, a Western Union memo said, "The telephone has too many shortcomings to be seriously considered as a means of communication. The device is inherently of no value to us."

- In 1943, the chairman of IBM announced that "There could not possibly be more than five people in the world who would want to own a computer."

- In 1927, H. M. Warner of Warner Brothers asked the question, "Who in the world wants to hear actors talk?"

- In the late-1930s, the noted movie actor Gary Cooper, talking about his decision to not take the lead role in the soon-to-be-released *Gone with the Wind*, said, "I'm just glad it'll be Clark Gable falling on his face, and not Gary Cooper."

• In 1899, Charles H. Duell, who was at that time the commissioner of the U.S. Patents Office, said, "Everything that can be invented has already been invented."

• And in 1962, the Decca Recording Company explained their decision to reject a new music group from England, the Beatles, by saying, "We don't like their sound, and besides, that guitar music is on the way out."

Now, of course, the common thread that runs through these famous sayings is *the danger of the closed mind*. We need to be ever open to new truth, as well as courageous enough sometimes to take a risk and try something new and different. Risk is what makes life exciting, and it is what makes life yield its fullest possibilities. It's an important element in what we call "the leap of faith."

And yet the truth is that many people today are afraid to try, afraid to step out, afraid to "throw deep" (if you'll forgive the football terminology!), afraid to risk, afraid to take the plunge, afraid to dive in. They live out their days in the prison of the closed mind.

There is an old story in the book of Second Kings that points to this. Recall it with me. Naaman was a great man, a national hero, a mighty warrior, a man of courage and power. He was highly successful—a respected military and political leader, captain of the king's guard in Syria, commander of the Syrian army. The people loved him. He had brought great victories to his nation. He was in high favor with the king. He was the king's right-hand man.

Naaman had it all. He was handsome, confident, wealthy, powerful, influential. But he developed a problem. The Scriptures record it bluntly. In 2 Kings 5:1, we find these words: "The man [Naaman], though a mighty warrior, suffered from leprosy."

An ever-increasing gloom settled on Naaman's household. Naaman was very sick, and daily his illness grew worse. Then a servant girl, a young Israelite, offered a possible solution. She remembered Elisha, the prophet in Israel, who sometimes healed people. Eventually, word that the prophet Elisha might be able to heal Naaman reached the king of Syria. Now, the king of Syria had no particular liking for prophets or preachers—especially those from Israel—but nonetheless, "Why not try it?" the king reasoned. "Naaman is so valuable; he is my chief servant. It is worth a try. What do we have to lose?"

The king moved quickly, commanding Naaman, "Go. I will send a royal letter [announcing your coming] to the king of Israel." Kings are like that. They like to throw their weight around. They negotiate from power. They have more trust in coercion than persuasion. And so in a few days, there rolled out of the city gate an impressive parade. Naaman, the national hero, was in the lead, followed by chariots and horses and men, and wagons loaded with servants and with lucrative bags of gold.

Off Naaman went to Israel with the hope that somehow he could find a cure for this terrible disease that was so drastically taking over his life. He had the king's letter in his hand, money in his pocket to buy the cure, and an entourage of servants to impress upon everyone that he was worthy of it. After all, he was a great man, and people should take note of that!

But then came the letdown. Then came the disappointment. They did not pay much attention to him in Israel. First of all, the king of Israel was suspicious of the whole thing. He didn't feel capable of healing anybody, and he didn't like the idea of the Syrian king giving him an ultimatum, so quickly the king of Israel hustled Naaman off to the prophet Elisha, distancing himself from the entire situation. But then the prophet Elisha didn't exactly roll out the red carpet either. He was busy with other matters. In fact, Elisha did not even come out of his house to meet Naaman—didn't even see the bags of gold and the magnificent parade of servants and wagons and chariots and soldiers. Elisha, because he was too busy to come out himself, instead sent out a servant (of all things!) with a ludicrous, ridiculous-sounding suggestion: "Go, Naaman, and wash in the Jordan River seven times, and you will be made well."

To put it mildly, none of this set well with Naaman. Didn't they realize who he was, how important he was? Naaman didn't like it. He didn't like this lackluster reception. He didn't like the prescription he had been given for his illness. He didn't want to "take the plunge" into the muddy old Jordan River! Didn't they realize that he was an exceptional man? a national hero? He wanted exceptional treatment and what he felt to be the proper respect.

Naaman got mad. It's interesting to watch a person get mad, especially if it's an anger fanned by pride. Here he was, Naaman—captain of the guard, chief commander, VIP—standing at the door of a poor Hebrew prophet, and the prophet wouldn't even come out to see him! And then, to top it all off, the prophet has sent a *servant* out to tell him to go wash himself in the Jordan. Of *all* rivers; the *Jordan*! That muddy, old river! Why, compared to the beautiful rivers in his home country, the Jordan looked like a drainage ditch!

The great man Naaman turned away in frustration, and he almost missed his moment. Offended, he turned away, proud, irate, arrogant, and indignant. He turned and, filled with disappointment, resolved to head back toward Syria. But, again, a servant spoke common sense to him: "But, sir, if the prophet had asked you to do some great thing, wouldn't you have done it? Wouldn't you have tried it? Why not try this? What have we got to lose? What could it hurt to try?"

Naaman cooled down a bit. He swallowed his pride, he seized the moment, and he did it. He "took the plunge"! Humbly, obediently, trusting and hoping, he did it. He went down into the muddy old waters of the Jordan, and he came out clean and whole and made well!

Isn't that a great story? Great because it's like a parable for us, for our time, for our own sickness. Because we, like Naaman, want to be well; we want to be whole, but we look for healing in all the wrong places. We refuse to "take the plunge" and try the one thing that will bring healing and make us well—humble, obedient, trusting, loving faith in God. This is too often true, for us as individuals and as a nation. Why is that? Why do people so fear the "leap of faith"? Why are people so afraid, so hesitant, so reluctant to "take the plunge"? Let me suggest some reasons. I'm sure you will think of others.

First, There Is Pride

To take the plunge into faith, you have to swallow your pride.

A few years ago, my friend Mark Trotter put it like this:

> Naaman is a perfect example for us, because he shows us that it's pride that stands between us and what God

wants for us. Pride, according to the Bible, is trying to order life the way we want it, according to our specifications, arranging things and other people, so that it is the way we want it to be—ignoring the facts and the other people who stand in our way.

Pride is what keeps us from salvation, according to the Bible. It keeps us from the life that God wants for us.

We say that if life is not the way we want it to be—if it's not the way we have ordered, then we won't accept it. If it's not offered to us on our terms we would rather be miserable, like Naaman, perched on his high horse—medals and armor weighing him down, servants and aides propping him up, a hundred victories behind him—evidence that he's got control of things in this life. He doesn't have to humble himself to anybody (or so he thinks). But there is still that one thing he can't control. Just one thing, but it's killing him. So, he risks humiliation, gets off his high horse, takes off his armor and his medals, leaves behind all those who support him, and alone—all alone—[he "just dives in," "takes the plunge"]—jumps into the river.

You know, don't you, that it wasn't the river that cured Naaman? That river was more likely to give you a disease than cure you of one. What cured Naaman was taking off all that pride and humbling himself. That's when he was made whole." [That's when God healed him.] (Mark Trotter, "Get Off Your High Horse," First United Methodist Church, San Diego, June 1, 1986.)

This all makes me wonder: How many people today are imprisoned by pride? How many want to set something right or clean something up? How many have one thing in their life that they can't control, one thing that's pulling them down and tearing them apart like a spiritual leprosy? How many want to make a profession of faith for the first time or ask for forgiveness or make a new start or join the church? And yet because of pride, they (like Naaman) turn away and go back to the same old life, the same old sickness.

Let me ask you something: Is your pride standing in your way, paralyzing you, immobilizing you, keeping you from taking the "leap of faith" you need to take? If so, "take it off"; take off the medals and the armor and the airs. Humble yourself and seize the moment. Do it today! Get off your high horse and plunge into the muddy old waters of the river Jordan, and God will make you fresh, clean, and whole.

That's the first idea I want to place before you. Many people today don't take the plunge into faith because of pride.

Second, There Is Procrastination

Can you imagine something like this going on in Naaman's mind: *Wash in the Jordan River? Now? At this moment, in front of all these* people? *A man of my stature? It would be so embarrassing to do such a thing in front of my soldiers and my servants!*

No! I can't do it! Not now! We'll go back to Syria, and then, maybe later, when no one is looking, I could slip back here and do this privately. Yes. That's *the answer: I will do it* later. *Maybe next week, or the week after that; or better still, next month, or perhaps next summer, or, come to think of it,* fall *might be better. Not now. I* can't *do it now. Maybe later.*

Can you relate to this? The truth is, most of us can because most of us have become quite proficient at the art of procrastination; we have become quite adept at the art of putting off and putting off and putting off. I saw an announcement recently. It said "National Procrastination Week will be held in February, or March, or April, or May, or perhaps in June." Upon reading this, I thought of the noted theologian Martin Marty and his "Parable of the Procrastinator." Have you heard this? Satan has called a meeting in Hades to receive reports from three of his workers. They want to conquer the world for evil and are strategizing as to the best way to accomplish their plan.

The first worker says, "Send me to the world, Satan. I will tell them there is no God."

Hearing this, Satan scowls and says, "That's been tried before."

The second worker says, "Send me to the world, Satan. I will tell them there is no sin."

Again, Satan scowls and says, "That's been tried before."

The third worker (who was smarter than the others) says, "Send me to the world, Satan. I will tell them 'there is no hurry!' "

Hearing this, Satan smiled and nodded his approval.

If you have something you need to do or say or fix, don't put it off any longer. It is urgent that you take care of it today.

Some fail to take the plunge into faith because of pride. Others fail because of procrastination.

Third and Finally, There Is Fear

Although Naaman was a brave and courageous man, even though he was a celebrated military hero, noted for his strength and valor and power, I'm sure that this situation struck fear deep down in his heart—a fear the likes of which he had never known before. Naaman had leprosy, and you can't defeat leprosy with a bow or a spear or a sword. You can't wrestle it to the ground and make it say "uncle." And now this suggestion from a poor Hebrew prophet about washing in the Jordan River added to the dilemma, added to the frustration, added to the fear. *What if it doesn't work? I will be humiliated. I'll look like a fool before my subjects. But worse, I will lose all hope,* Naaman must have reasoned within.

But then he decided to stop trying to control the situation. He worked through the fear, and in trust he walked down into the river, and then the miracle happened: He was healed, he was cleansed, and he was made well!

In his book *Believe and Belong* ([Old Tappan, N.J.: Power Books, 1982], p. 21), Bruce Larson uses an analogy that makes the point. He tells about the gigantic statue of Atlas in the entrance of the RCA Building on Fifth Avenue in New York City. There is Atlas, struggling and straining and holding the world on his shoulders. "Now that's one way to live," says Bruce Larson, "trying to carry the world on your shoulders." On the other side of Fifth Avenue, Larson reminds us, is Saint Patrick's Cathedral. There, behind the high altar, is a small statue of Jesus as a little boy—about eight or nine years old—and with no effort at all, he is holding the whole world in one hand.

Bruce Larson says, "We have a choice. We can carry the world on our shoulders or we can say, 'I give up, Lord, here's my life. I give You my world, the whole world.'"

The point is clear: We have to get past the pride, past the procrastination, past the fear before we can take the plunge into faith and find the healing we so desperately need. Whatever you do, don't miss the "leap of faith"!

❧ 11 ❧
Don't Miss . . .
The Priorities of Life

Scripture: Joshua 24:14-15

Recently, one of our church's college students sent to me a wonderful story about the importance of keeping our priorities straight. The story is about a time-management expert, who was speaking to a group of business students one day. As the expert stood before this class of high-powered overachievers, he said, "Okay, time for a quiz." He brought out a one-gallon, widemouthed Mason jar and set it on a table in front of him. Then he produced about a dozen fist-sized rocks and carefully placed them, one at a time, into the jar. When the jar was filled to the top and no more of the big rocks would fit inside, he asked, "Is the jar full?"

Everyone in the class said, "Yes."

The speaker replied, in a sly manner, "Really?" He reached under the table and pulled out a bucket of gravel. Then he dumped some gravel in and shook the jar, causing pieces of gravel to work themselves down into the spaces between the big rocks. Then he smiled and asked the group once more, "Is the jar full now?"

By this time, the class was getting the picture, and one of the students answered, "Probably not."

"Good!" he replied. He then reached under the table, and this time he brought out a bucket of sand. He started dumping the sand into the jar, and it went into all the spaces left between the big rocks and the gravel.

Once more he asked the class, "What do you think? Is the jar full now?"

"No!" the class shouted.

Once again he said, "Good!" and then he grabbed a pitcher of water and began to pour it in until the jar was filled to the brim. Then, he looked up at the class and asked, "What is the point of this demonstration?"

One eager student raised his hand and said, "The point is, no matter how full your schedule is, if you try really hard, you can always work some more things into it."

"No," the expert said, "that's not the point. What we have here is a life lesson we dare not forget, namely this: If you don't put the big rocks in first, you'll never get them in at all!" (Adapted from Stephen Covey, et al., *First Things First* [New York: Simon & Schuster, 1994], pp. 88-89.)

Wasn't that a great lesson to give to those students "If you don't put the big rocks in first, you'll never get them in at all." This serves as a reminder to us to focus on the real priorities—the "big rocks," the key things—first, because in the hectic pace of this life, if you don't work them in early, they will likely get left out altogether. But of course, the question is What are the big rocks of life for *you*? What are the real priorities for you? What do you give your time and effort and energy to first? What are the most urgent, crucial commitments for you?

This is precisely what the message in Joshua 24 is all about. Remember how forcefully Joshua said it: "Choose this day whom you will serve . . . but as for me and my household, we will serve the LORD" (24:15). This is one of the greatest statements in the entire Bible. It has resounded like a trumpet fanfare across the ages. If you wanted to memorize some key verses of Scripture, this would be a pretty good place to start. "Choose this day whom you will serve . . . but as for me and my household, we will serve the LORD." But what was the context of this? What prompted Joshua to make this great statement? If you listen closely, you can hear a strong commitment in his words, but also a tone of exasperation.

You see, after all those years of wandering in the wilderness, the Hebrews had now come into the promised land. They had dreamed of this. They had longed for this. They had prayed for this. But now that they were in the land, they had a big problem: other people lived in this land too, and these other people had their own set of gods that they worshiped. They had a god of war, and a god of wine, and a god of fertility, and a god of this, and a god of that, and a god of the other. And some of these false gods apparently were attractive to the Hebrews.

In fact, some of these false gods were so enticing to the Hebrews that they actually began worshiping them instead of worshiping the Lord, and this, of course, was a blatant violation of the first commandment. Joshua saw what the Hebrew people were doing, and bravely, boldly, dramatically, he said, "Choose this day whom you will serve, whether the gods your ancestors served in the region beyond the River or the gods of the Amorites in whose land you are living; but as for me and my household, we will serve the LORD." Joshua's strong words here remind me of the man who boarded an airplane one evening. The flight attendant asked him if he would like dinner.

The man asked, "What are my choices?"

The attendant answered, "Yes or no!"

When it comes to God, those are our choices—yes or no. We can't sit on the fence; can't skirt the issue. We have to decide—yes or no. Do we accept God into our lives or not? Do we commit our lives to God or not? Do we put God first or not?

This story in Joshua 24 is about choices, decisions, commitments, and priorities. Let me bring this closer to home and encourage you to think through what *your* priorities are right now. What are the "big rocks" in your life? If you don't put those in first, you will never get them in at all. Let me suggest three priorities that we would all do well to embrace as we live out our days.

First of All, There Is Commitment to Christ

Talk about a big rock: Jesus Christ is the "Rock of Ages"!

Recently, I ran across a series of humorous stories from pastors across the country. Jim Cobb of First Lutheran Church in Norfolk, Virginia, tells about a young woman who married just after she completed college. Apparently, she was still in the "multiple-choice" testing mode, because when asked "Do you take this man for better or worse, for richer or poorer, in sickness and in health?" she replied, "I'll pick *better, richer,* and *health*!"

Dan Johnson of Kalaska Church of Christ in Kalaska, Michigan, asked recently: "Did you hear about the neurotic owl that said 'Why? Why?'"

Berkley Helms, pastor of Grace Baptist Church in Sarasota, Florida, tells of a man who bumped into a buddy of his at the golf course. He noticed that both of his buddy's ears were bandaged. "Cecil, what happened?" the man asked. Cecil replied, "Well, I was ironing a shirt when the phone rang. Accidentally I put the iron up to my ear instead of the phone." Curious, his friend asked, "So what happened to the other ear?" Cecil replied, "He called back!"

And Leonard Pye, minister of the Highland Community Church in Highland, Illinois, recently said this: "Regarding original sin, Adam blamed Eve, Eve blamed the serpent, [and] the serpent didn't have a leg to stand on." (Thanks to Michael Brown, *Through Centenary Windows* 15, no. 42 [November 5, 1998], Winston-Salem Centenary United Methodist Church.)

Now, the good news for us as Christians is that we have something better than a leg to stand on. We have a rock! Remember how the hymn writer put it: "On Christ the solid rock I stand, / all other ground is sinking sand" (Edward Mote, "My Hope Is Built"). Dr. William B. McClain is the professor of preaching and worship at Wesley Theological Seminary. Dr. McClain once told about meeting a South Korean tailor in Seoul, Korea. Amazingly, this tailor introduced himself as "Smitty Lee." Dr. McClain was fascinated to discover a Korean named Smitty, and he asked whether the name Smitty was a Korean name. The Korean tailor said no, and then he told the story of how his life had been saved some years before, during the Korean War, by a courageous American soldier from Virginia, who was called Smitty Ransom. The tailor went on to explain a rather familiar custom in that Asian culture, summing it up in two simple sentences: "He saved my life. I took his name."

This is precisely what happens when Jesus Christ comes into our hearts. He saves our lives. And we take his name. We take on the name *Christian*, one who is "of Christ," one who follows Christ, one who belongs to Christ, one who serves Christ. But sometimes we get busy and distracted, and we lose our focus and forget our name. We get so involved with the gravel and the sand and the small, petty rocks of life, and sadly, we drift away from the Rock of Ages. If we don't put the big rocks in first, we'll never get them in at all.

How is it with you right now? Are you wearing the

name of Christ well? Do you bring honor to his name by the way you live? Is your life a grateful tribute to him? Or are you chasing after the latest fads, the newest false gods? How about it: Are you putting Christ first in your life? Are you? "Choose this day whom you will serve . . . but as for me and my household, we will serve the LORD" by making commitment to Christ our top priority.

Second, There Is Commitment to Family

Joshua said, "As for me and my household . . . " Family was obviously a priority for him.

A young man was at the airport in Portland, Oregon, waiting for a friend to deplane. Right beside him, also waiting for someone to deplane, was a young woman with a little baby in her arms and two small boys at her side. They were waiting for her husband, the children's father.

And when he came out of the jetway and spotted them, his face lit up. He ran to them, put down his bag, picked up one of his sons, and gave him a great big hug. "It's so good to see you, Son! I've really missed you," the man said. And the little boy said, "And I've really missed you, too, Dad."

Then the man picked up his older son and gave him a big hug, and said, "My goodness, you are getting so big! I can't believe how fast you are growing. What a wonderful young man you are. I'm so proud of you!"

Next, he reached for his baby daughter. "Hi, Angel!" he said softly. "How is Daddy's favorite girl in all the world?" The baby girl smiled and put her head down on her daddy's strong shoulder.

Then, the man said, "Now, for the best of all!" He reached out and embraced his wife. He hugged her tightly and said, "I love you so much. I am the luckiest guy in the world to have you!" Adoringly, they looked into each other's eyes, beaming with big smiles of delight and affection and joy.

The young man who was waiting for his friend watched this family reunion with envy. "Wow!" he said out loud. "How long have you two been married?" The man answered: "Fourteen years, and we are so happy together."

Then the young man asked, "How long have you been away?" thinking it must have been weeks or maybe even months. Given their warm expressions of affection, he was surprised when the man answered, "Two days." The young man couldn't believe it. Two days; just two days, and they all greeted one another like this.

Then the young man said, "You have so much love and joy in your family. I hope someday I can have a family like that."

The man looked him straight in the eye and said, "Don't just hope, my friend, *decide!*"

Whatever shape or size our family may be, we can decide to work at it. We can decide to give our best to it. We can decide to make our family a priority. In all of my years in the ministry, I have stood beside a lot of deathbeds, and I want to tell you, over all this time, I have never once heard someone on his or her deathbed say, "I sure wish I had spent more time at the office." That's not what they say. They say, "I wish I had spent more time with my children," or, "I wish I had given more time to my spouse," or, "I wish I had visited Mother [or called Dad] more." *That's* what they say—not "I wish I had spent more time at the office."

"Choose this day whom you will serve...but as for me and my household, we will serve the LORD" by making commitment to Christ and commitment to family top priorities in life.

Third and Finally, There Is
Commitment to the Church

This too is what Joshua was talking about. He was saying to his people, "Well, what are you going to do? Are
you going to be God's church or not? Are you going to be
God's people or not? Are you going to make the church a
priority in your life or not?"

A minister friend of mine recently wrote a letter to a
family in his church. The family had been very active at
one time, but he hadn't seen them lately and was concerned, so he wrote to them to say that he was missing
them and hoped that they were not unhappy with him or
with the church. A few days later, he received a haunting
letter that went something like this:

Dear Pastor,

Thank you for your kind letter. And, yes, we haven't
been in church for several months now, so maybe we
should explain. In the summer, we go to the lake every
weekend. Our kids are young now, and it's so important
that they learn how to water-ski and become expert
skiers. And we like to get away too, Jack and me, because
there's so much going on in our lives and we just need a
break.

But then when summer's over, soccer begins and our
kids all play in the most competitive leagues. They have
games every weekend, and sometimes the games are out
of town, and when they are in town, we go to the soccer
games either on Saturday or Sunday, and there is just no
way we can make it to church.

We will be back to church. Don't give up on us. There's
a brief period of time when soccer is over, and basketball
hasn't yet begun, and it's too cold to go to the lake, and
that's a great time for us to go to church. But, then again,

118

it's Christmas, and you know how hectic that is. And after Christmas we just have to go to Colorado to ski, so that time's got a problem too.

But one of these days, don't be surprised when you look up and see us out there in the congregation, because we just love you, and we just love our church.

When I read that letter, I couldn't help thinking of Joshua and his strong words: "Choose this day whom you will serve...but as for me and my household, we will serve the LORD." Why? Because there are a whole lot of "false gods" in our culture today that are not that different from the false gods the Hebrews faced in the promised land. Their names are soccer, and football, and basketball. Their names are golf, and fishing, and sleeping in, and shopping, and getting a head start on my yard work. Their names are money, and social status.

Please don't misunderstand me. There's nothing wrong with any of these things in and of themselves. I love soccer and football and baseball and golf. There is nothing wrong with these things, as long as they don't take the place of God and God's sovereignty in our lives.

So, the point is this: Whether we like it or not, we have to make a decision. Will we be loyal to God or not? Will we put God first or not? Will we serve God or something else? "Choose this day whom you will serve...but as for me and my household, we will serve the LORD" by making commitment to Christ, commitment to family, and commitment to the church our top priorities. If we don't put the "big rocks" in first, we will never get them in at all.

❧ 12 ❧
Don't Miss . . .
The Joy of Service

Scripture: 1 Corinthians 12:27-31

During Jesus' time on this earth, three of his closest friends were Martha, Mary, and Lazarus. Martha, you may remember, was the woman who worked so hard to prepare meals for Jesus and his followers. Mary, you may recall, was Martha's sister who anointed Jesus with perfume and wiped his feet with her hair (see Luke 10:38-42). Lazarus was their brother, whom Jesus raised from the dead (see John 11).

Max Lucado, in his book *A Gentle Thunder: Hearing God Through the Storm* ([Dallas: Word Publishing, 1995], pp. 126-27), likens these three very different personalities to instruments in a band. Martha, he sees as representing the drum. She is a worker, an organizer, a "Type A" personality, one who sets the pace, one who takes charge, one who rolls up her sleeves and gets the job done. She is what we would call a "no-nonsense, practical person." The primary focus and emphasis of life for Martha is on *doing*—beating the drum of service.

Mary, on the other hand, Max Lucado likens to the flute. She is soft, gentle, and soulful. She is a dreamer who is deeply spiritual and worshipful, committed to prayer and praise, and spiritual growth and formation. The primary focus and emphasis of Mary's life is on *being*—playing the flute of celebration.

Lazarus, whom Jesus raised from the dead, had such a powerful, incredible story to share and tell that Max Lucado appropriately sees him as a trumpet, trumpeting to the world the good news of Christ's love and power. Lazarus is a person of testimony and witness, sharing with everyone he can the grace and new life that he has received from Jesus. The primary focus and emphasis of life for Lazarus is on *witnessing*—on trumpeting the story.

Though siblings, though part of the same family, each of these three persons was unique. Each one had his or her role to play; together they played the music of the gospel. God gave each of them a special gift to use for his Kingdom. God gave Martha a bass drum for service. God gave Mary a flute for praise. God gave Lazarus a trumpet for testimony and witness.

The point of the analogy is clear, namely this: Each and every one of us has been given an instrument to play in Christ's church, and each one is essential and important. Some of us are drums; like Martha, we are doers. Some of us are flutes; like Mary, we are pray-ers. Some of us are trumpets; like Lazarus, we share the good news of God's love and power with words and deeds. We are all important, and we all need one another. We are all different from one another, but when we blend our differences and work together, God can accomplish great things through us. But the question is, What is *your* instrument? And are you *playing* it?

This is precisely what the apostle Paul is talking about in 1 Corinthians 12. In fact, he spells it out for us! Paul says, "Now, you are the body of Christ and individually members of it. And God has appointed in the church first apostles, second prophets, third teachers; then deeds of power, then gifts of healing, forms of assistance, forms of leadership, various kinds of tongues. Are all apostles? Are all prophets? Are all teachers? . . . But strive for the greater gifts" (verses 27-31a). Then Paul adds this fascinating sentence: "And I will show you a still more excellent way" (verse 31b). What does this mean? What is the "still more excellent way" that Paul is talking about here? Well, if you keep on reading, you will see that his very next words are found in 1 Corinthians 13, which is often called "the love chapter." What the apostle Paul is saying is this: Find your special gift. Find your unique talent. Find your instrument in God's band, and play it in the spirit of love.

If you will forgive me, I want to be very personal with you. I would like to tell you a little something about my own personal faith journey. I could mention a hundred or more conversations that have touched my life in some way, but I would like to share with you three particular conversations that helped me find my unique instrument in God's orchestra. These three conversations helped shape who I am and how I personally try to serve God through the church. And in my sharing with you a little something of my own spiritual pilgrimage, maybe you will be able to find yourself and your own special way of serving somewhere between the lines.

Conversation Number One

This conversation happened on a Saturday morning in Lexington, Tennessee, some years ago. I had just graduated from seminary, had just been ordained an elder, and had just received my first full-time appointment, as pastor of the Milledgeville-Morris Chapel Charge in the Memphis Conference. Our family moved into the parsonage on a Thursday, and the following Saturday morning I went to my first district ministers' meeting. We were having coffee, standing around visiting before the meeting, when I saw Kenneth Stewart coming toward me. He approached me and smiled. We shook hands, and he said, "Aren't you Jim Moore?"

"Yes."

"Well, I've heard about you, and after the meeting, we're going to go down to the corner drugstore and get some coffee, because I want to ask you a question."

Now, I was amazed that Kenneth Stewart knew my name. How did he know anything about me? Kenneth was probably in his midforties at the time, and he was something of a legend in West Tennessee because he was a maverick. He was independently wealthy. His family owned a number of shopping centers. He didn't have to work at all, but he felt called by God to be a pastor, and he loved to preach, and so he did. His financial situation, however, gave him an interesting, unusual, sometimes off-the-wall way of looking at things. He was not beholden to the system.

All through that meeting, I kept wondering: *What in the world does Kenneth Stewart want to ask me?* Later that morning, we walked down to the drugstore coffee shop. We sipped our coffee, and Kenneth Stewart looked over his glasses at me and made me feel nervous. Finally, he said, "Are you ready for the question?"

"Yes sir," I answered.

"Well," he said, "The question is: What are you going to do?"

I responded, "Kenneth, I'm not sure how to answer that, because I don't know where you are coming from."

"I want to know," he said "what you are going to do with your ministry."

"Kenneth," I said, "I still don't know what you mean."

"Let me help you," he said. "The question is: Are you going to marry the local church or are you going to marry the system? Right now, you are young, and you think you can do both, and to some extent you can, and that's all right. But, at some point, you have to decide, Where is my first loyalty? Where is my first priority? Where is my number one commitment? What will I give my best energy to—the local church or the system? Now, if you still don't understand what I'm talking about, let me put it like this. There are two kinds of ministers: There are those who endure the year just to get to go to annual conference, and there are those who celebrate the year and endure annual conference! Which one of these are you going to be?"

Now, let me hurry to say that we need *both* of those kinds of ministers—those who serve the system well, and those who serve the local church well. They are both valid, and they are both needed. But I personally decided to give my life to the local church. Now, I serve the system and do the best I can with that, but my real love is in the local church, in St. Luke's. Here is where the action is for me. This is what I feel called and equipped to do. The local church is what excites me and thrills me and challenges me and inspires me. Some people get up in the morning and go to bed at night thinking about the system. I get up in the morning and go to bed at night thinking about the local church.

Now, you are probably wondering what in the world does this have to do with you. Actually, it has a lot to do with you, because, you see, *you* have to make this decision too! Where are you going to serve God—in the system of society or through the local church? I have eight letters on my desk right now (they just keep coming) in which I have been asked to serve in some system of our society—a social organization, a fraternal organization, a civic organization, and I could go on and on. And I do those things and enjoy them, but never to the detriment of my church, because I decided long ago to marry the local church—to serve other organizations as I can, trying to be the church out in society, but to always put my church first.

A great example of this was Eddy Scurlock. Mr. Eddy was one of the early pioneers who helped start the church I pastor, St. Luke's, in Houston. Mr. Eddy served his city and his community in amazing ways, but a hundred times or more I heard him say this: "My church comes first, and then I'll do what I can." Every time he was honored or interviewed (and he was honored and interviewed a lot), he would work that theme into the conversation. "I'm glad to do what I can, but my church comes first."

Now, please don't misunderstand me. One of the things I love most about St. Luke's is how our members go out to "be the church" in the city and how they give strong Christian leadership in the community. I try to do my part out there too, but I want you to know that the reason I decided with Mr. Eddy that "my church comes first" is because the church has Jesus Christ. The world is starving to death for Jesus Christ, and we have him! No other institution or movement or organization in the world has anything that even comes close or that even begins to compare with Jesus Christ. That's what we are about. That's the bottom line. We are here to share Jesus Christ with a needy world, and everything we do is for that purpose. And that's why I decided to give my best to the local church, to make that the priority and to make that my main place of service for Christ.

Have you made that decision? I have; that's a big part of who I am, and it affects most every decision I make.

Conversation Number Two

This conversation took place some years ago in a McDonald's restaurant. I had just gone to work in a church that had a state-of-the-art television studio, and I had been asked to figure out new ways to use television to proclaim the Christian faith. I didn't know the first thing about television—I had no training and no experience. I tried to bluff it for a while, but that didn't work, so I went over to the local television affiliate—our worship services were broadcast on their network each Sunday—and found a seasoned veteran of television named John. I persuaded him to help me. He was great and was so patient with me, and before long we were using television in a variety of ways: telecasting our morning worship services, radio broadcasting our evening service, creating Sunday school television series, developing TV teaching aids for the annual conference, and I was even doing a faith-based talk show.

But much earlier on, when all of this was still unknown to me and I was really feeling in over my head with the task of figuring out how to use the technology we had available, I took my TV friend John to lunch under the Golden Arches, and I said to him, "John, teach me how to do television. Tell me what is the most important thing I need to know about producing a TV program." I'll never forget his answer. It changed my life. He said, "Jim, when you start to produce a television program, you have to decide this first—you have to first answer this question: 'Do I want to broadcast or narrowcast my message?'"

And I said, "John, I don't have the faintest idea what you are talking about."

He said, "Well, let me put it like this: To *broad*cast is to aim your message toward the masses of the people. To *narrow*cast is to aim your message at a small, focused group of people. Both types of message are legitimate, and both are needed, but you have to decide which one you want to do before you start, because that decision will dictate everything else you do thereafter."

"For example," he said, "we produced a video for the annual conference where you interviewed the bishop about pension benefits for ministers in Louisiana. He did a good job. You did a good job, but it was narrowcasting because 99.9 percent of the world couldn't care less about pension benefits for preachers in Louisiana. And recently, we did that video series for Sunday school on "What United Methodists Believe Today." It was well done and well received in the adult Sunday school classes, but it was narrowcasting, because, believe it or not, I bet there was not one person in our city who was lying in bed last night tossing and turning and wondering, *Man, I wonder what those Methodists believe!"*

John explained further, "Narrowcasting is all right if that's what you want to do, but to reach the masses of the people, you have to *broad*cast. You have to speak to the cries of the people. You have to meet them where they are. You have to speak their language."

That conversation changed my life, because (among other things) it changed my approach to preaching. I don't want to *narrow*cast the gospel. I want to *broad*cast it! I want to hear the cries of the people and speak to their hurts and to their questions in language they can understand. That's why I don't preach sermons on "Eighth-century B.C. Prophets: What They Thought About Eschatology, and Its Theological and Existential Implications." Nobody I know of is losing sleep over that topic.

One time at a party, a woman said to me, "Jim, I love to hear you preach, because you are so simple!" I loved that comment! I took it as a compliment, because she was telling me that I am *broad*casting the gospel. People tease me about my "three-point sermons," but there is a reason why I do them. People tease me about all of my stories and illustrations, but there is a reason why I share them. I am trying my best to "broadcast" the Christian faith in language and in images that a great number of the people can understand and can relate to and can find helpful.

What do I hope this says to you? Simply this: Ask yourself, How can I, in my life, broadcast the gospel? As a parent or grandparent, as a Sunday school teacher or any kind of teacher, as a coworker or as a friend, how do you hear the cries of people, the questions of people, the hurts of people, and then broadcast the Christian faith in ways they can hear and understand, and from which they can find strength for the living of these days?

Conversation Number Three

This conversation took place on a Monday morning in Dr. D. L. Dykes's office at First United Methodist Church in Shreveport, Louisiana, twenty years ago. I was visiting with D. L. when suddenly one of our young associate ministers came into the office and said, "D. L. and Jim, I'm going to resign from the staff and go back to Oklahoma. D. L.," he said, "I came down here so you could teach me to preach, but I realize that you don't have time to teach me, so I am going back home."

D. L. said to him, "You want me to teach you how to preach? Sit down there for a moment, and tell me what you wanted to say in that sermon you preached last night."

The young man said, "Well, I wanted to say [this and that and the other]."

D. L. said, "Very good, but let me ask you something. Why didn't you say that?"

That was the greatest lesson on preaching I have ever heard. Five words: "Why didn't you say that?" The young man the night before had preached a sermon with high-sounding theological gobbledygook, and nobody knew what he was talking about. He had quoted German theologians in a pontificating voice, and people had sat there with blank faces.

D. L. paused for a moment, and then he said to the young man, "You know, I went through that too. I used to carry so many books home at night I was spilling them everywhere." And then he said, "I made a great discovery—I discovered, amazingly, that God had put a well of living water in me, and that's what I needed to talk about— *my* experience with the text, not Karl Barth's or Paul Tillich's or Reinhold Niebuhr's."

D. L. said, "I still read the writings of those great minds, but when I get ready to write, I clear my desk of everything but my Bible and my legal pad, and then I ask one question: What does this text say to me? What does this Bible passage say to the well of living water in me, and how can I share that message with others from my heart?"

What a great thought that is! Every single one of us has within us a well of living water. There is within us a well of living water that can be expressed through the drum of active service like Martha, or through the flute of quiet prayer like Mary, or through the trumpet of powerful witness like Lazarus.

Now, let me ask you something. How is it with *you* right now? Are you really supporting the church with your prayers, with your presence, with your gifts, and with your service? One thing is for sure: God has a special job for you, a special instrument he wants you to play. The question is, Have you found it? And will you play it?

Don't miss it. Don't miss the joy of your unique service.

❧ 13 ❧
Don't Miss . . .
The Spirit of Compassion

Scripture: Matthew 25:31-40

John Powell, in his devotional book *Through Seasons of the Heart* ([Allen, Tex.: Tabor Publishing, 1987], pp. 233-34) shares a fascinating Irish legend. Read closely, if you will, "The Legend of the King Who Had No Children." Once upon a time there was a country whose beloved king had no children and, consequently, no heir to the throne, no successor. To deal with this problem, the king devised a plan. He sent out his messengers to post signs on the trees in all the towns of his kingdom. The signs announced that every qualified young person should apply for an interview with the king as a possible successor to the throne. However, all such applicants must have two special qualifications: (1) they must love God; and (2) they must love their fellow human beings.

In one small village, one young man saw the signs and reflected that he did "indeed love God and his fellow human beings," and he wanted to go to the king's castle for an interview. However, there was a problem. The young man was so poor that he had no clothes that would be presentable in the sight of the king. Nor did he have the money to buy provisions he would need to make the journey to the castle. So he worked and begged and borrowed until, at long last, he had enough money to buy the appropriate clothes and the necessary provisions. Finally, he set out for the castle.

He had almost completed his journey—the castle was in sight—when he came upon a poor beggar by the side of the road. The beggar sat there trembling, clad only in rags. The beggar pleadingly extended his arms and held out his hands for help. In a weak voice, he quietly said, "I'm hungry. I'm thirsty. I'm weak. I'm cold. Would you please help me?" The young man was so moved, so touched with compassion by the need of the poor beggar, that he immediately stripped off his new clothes and gave them to the beggar, and the young man put on the beggar's own rags. Without a second thought, he gave the beggar all of his food and money—all of his provisions. It was clear that this young man loved God, and he loved his fellow human beings. Then the young man proceeded somewhat uncertainly to the castle, wearing the rags of the beggar and without any provisions for his journey home. He thought to himself, *This is probably a waste of time now. Dressed in these rags, they won't pay any attention to me at all. They may not even let me in the castle.*

However, upon his arrival at the castle, an attendant to the king welcomed him warmly and showed him in. After a long wait, he was finally admitted to the throne room of the king. Humbly, he bowed before his king. When he looked up into the face of the king, he could not believe his eyes. He was filled with astonishment. "Oh, my king," he said, "you were the beggar by the side of the road!"

"Yes," replied the king, "I was the beggar."

"But you are not really a beggar. You are really the king. Why did you trick me? Why did you do this to me?" the young man asked.

"Because I had to find out if you really do love—if you

really do love God and your fellow human beings. I knew that if I came to you as king, you would have been very much impressed by my crown of gold and my regal robes, and you would have tried to impress me. You would have done anything I asked because of my kingly appearance and power. But that way, I would never have known what is really in your heart. So I came to you as a beggar, with no claims on you except for the love in your heart. And I have found out that you truly do love God and your fellow human beings. You will be my successor! You will inherit my kingdom!"

Isn't that a beautiful legend? But wait a minute! Haven't we heard this story before? I don't know who originally created the legend, but whoever did surely was inspired to write it by Jesus' parable of the great judgment in Matthew 25. Remember in that classic parable, how all the nations are gathered before the throne of God and some of the people are given a great blessing?

Come, you that are blessed by my Father, inherit the kingdom prepared for you from the foundation of the world; for I was hungry and you gave me food, I was thirsty and you gave me something to drink, I was a stranger and you welcomed me, I was naked and you gave me clothing, I was sick and you took care of me, I was in prison and you visited me. (verses 34-36)

But notice something here. Upon hearing this, the righteous are surprised (verse 37). This is one of my favorite parts of this story. Notice that they aren't arrogant or presumptuous or pompous or holier than thou. The righteous people are surprised. Not smug; *surprised!* "But wait, O gracious King! When? When did we see you hungry and feed you, and thirsty and give you drink? When did we see you a stranger and welcome you, and naked and clothe you? And when did we see you sick or in prison and visit you?" And the king gives that magnificent answer that resounds across the ages: "Truly I tell you, just as you did it to one of the least of these...you did it to me" (verse 40).

This parable shows us that the best way to love God is to love his children. This parable shows us how much it pleases God when we love and respect one another. This parable shows us that God wants us to bring the spirit of love and respect to everything we do. Everything we do, we should do it as if we are doing it for God. Let me show you what I mean.

First of All, As Christians We Bring This Spirit to the Way We Work

As Christians, we approach every task, every job, as if we were doing it for God. Will Willimon tells about a young man who had just finished law school and was anxious to begin his practice. He was invited for an interview with a very prestigious law firm. It was more than this young man could ever have hoped for. The interview went exceptionally well. He was put up in a first-class hotel. He was royally entertained. He really liked the lawyers he had met. They obviously liked him very much.

All was going great until the last moments of the interview, when one of the lawyers casually mentioned that one of their clients was a company that had a shady reputation. The company was known for making a great deal of money by taking advantage of poor and uneducated people. The young lawyer expressed reservations about representing a company that so blatantly took advantage of innocent people. He was quickly reassured by the other lawyers that everything that company did was perfectly legal. "It may be legal," replied the young lawyer, "but it is not ethical, and it is not right!"

Well, that ended the interview. The young lawyer returned home. A few days later, he learned that the law firm had moved in another direction in their search and had chosen someone else. Will Willimon said that his heart really went out to this young man. He had blown his chance to have the job he had always wanted and deserved. "Actually, I feel great," said the young lawyer. "I'm grateful that they gave me the opportunity to clarify who I am and what I really want from my law practice. I'm OK. I now have a much better idea of the kind of law I want to practice. I feel sorry for them because I know that many of them feel the same way I feel, but they are trapped in the system and can't get out."

Will Willimon was touched and impressed by the maturity and strong character of that young lawyer, and Will asked him, "What makes you so confident, so bold to live your life in this way?" I love the young lawyer's answer. He said, "I'm a Christian! I'm not just living my life on the basis of what I want, or just by what seems right to me. I'm trying to live my life based on the principles of Christ" (Will Willimon, *Pulpit Resource* 27, no. 3 [July/August/September 1999]: 5).

That young man is on target, isn't he? He's trying to live out the truth of Matthew 25. He's bringing that spirit—"Do everything as if you were doing it for Christ"—right into the work arena. Sometimes when it comes to work, we forget to do that—to work as if we were working for Christ—and we can get our priorities mixed up. Over the years I have noticed that there are several different ways in which people approach their work. Someone put it like this: When it comes to work, some recline, some whine, and some shine.

The recliners are those who hate work, and they loaf through it as much as they can. They lie down on the job. The whiners are those who work grudgingly, resenting every minute of it and putting more energy into the complaining than the job itself. And then there are those who shine, those who approach their work and perform their work in a happy, productive, creative way. These people see their work as an opportunity to serve God and to improve the quality of life in this world.

Long before Robert Fulghum wrote his best-selling book *All I Really Need to Know I Learned in Kindergarten*, Charlie Brown had set forth his summary of life in a "Peanuts" cartoon strip that appeared in 1975. Charlie Brown's "Good Rules for Living" included the following:

1. Don't leave your crayons in the sun.
2. Use dental floss every day.
3. Don't spill the shoe polish.
4. Always knock before entering.
5. Don't let ants get into the sugar.
6. Never volunteer to be program chairman.
7. Always get your first serve in.

We like these kinds of lesson statements, which concisely summarize truths and meanings about life. Well, the apostle Paul, in his letter to the Colossians, gives us a great one—the magic key for how the Christian approaches work. He puts it like this: "Whatever your task, put yourselves into it, as done for the Lord and not for your masters" (Colossians 3:23). In other words, Paul was saying, put your whole heart into your work, as if you were doing it for Christ.

This is our calling as Christians—to bring this spirit of love and respect to our work. That's the key. That's the priority. We perform our job as though we are working for God. We work as unto the Lord.

Second, As Christians We Bring This Spirit to the Way We Speak

We need to learn how to speak to everyone we meet as if that person were Christ himself, in disguise. We need to speak with that kind of love and respect, as if that person we are addressing is none other than our Lord himself. When you stop and think about it, isn't it astonishing and sad how harshly some people speak these days? People who supposedly love one another—husbands and wives, parents and children, neighbors and friends—sometimes bash one another with hard, hateful words spewed out in a tone so hostile and cruel that it sounds profane and obscene.

Some years ago, I was working with a middle-aged couple who were having serious marital problems. One day the man said to me, "Sure, I talk tough to her, but she can take it. Everybody knows I was born with a hot temper. I say hard things to her all the time, but she knows how I am. She understands." And I had to tell him, "No, she doesn't! She doesn't understand! Again and again, day after day, week after week, she comes to the church, crying, and she keeps saying to me, 'Jim, how can he love me, and talk to me like that?'"

Oh, how we need help here! We need to learn how to speak words of love, not hatefulness; words of encouragement, not discouragement; words that build up, not words that tear down; and words that inspire, not words that deflate.

When it comes to the way we work and the way we speak, we need to do it as though it is for the Lord.

Third and Finally, As Christians We Bring This Spirit to the Way We Treat Others

I have a good friend who is one of the most outgoing, gregarious persons I have ever known. He is so full of life that he can light up a room. Physically, he is a great, big guy, a former football player, strong, powerful, and yet he has a "teddy bear" personality. He's a hugger. He just hugs everybody. He is wired up that way. He expresses his love with hugs. Some years ago I heard him speak to a group of young people, and he said something that inspired them and touched me. He said, "When I first became a Christian, I was so frustrated because I wanted to hug God and didn't know how." He said, "I was so thrilled by what God had done for me in Christ, I was so grateful for the way God had turned my life around, I wanted to hug God, but I didn't know how." And then he said this, "Over the years, I have learned that the best way to hug God is to hug his children; the best way to love God is to love his children; the best way to serve God is to serve his children."

He's right, you know. That's what Jesus' parable in Matthew 25 is all about. It reminds us that we should do everything as if we are doing it for God—the way we work, the way we speak, and, yes, the way we treat others. Everything we do, we do it as if we were doing it for our Lord. Jesus said, "As you did it to one of the least of these—you did it to me." Don't miss that! Don't miss the great spirit of love, respect, and compassion.

❧ 14 ❧
Don't Miss . . .
The Dramatic Lessons of Life

Scripture: Luke 19:41-44

Pearl, Mississippi. West Paducah, Kentucky. Jonesboro, Arkansas. Springfield, Oregon. Littleton, Colorado. These five towns have much in common. They are all nice, quiet towns highly representative of Middle America. They all typify the attractive, tranquil, suburban area—that is, safe and secure, pleasant for families, the kind of place you'd want to raise your kids. They are all the kinds of places to which many people intentionally move in order to get away from the hustle and bustle and violence of the big city.

But the common thread that dramatically links these five towns together can be found in the brutal and tragic fact that in each of these places, misguided, misdirected, mixed-up, crazed teenagers came into their schools with assault weapons and went on a killing rampage, mowing down their classmates and their teachers.

Pearl, Mississippi. West Paducah, Kentucky. Jonesboro, Arkansas. Springfield, Oregon. And Littleton, Colorado. These five towns show us graphically that what we don't know will hurt us.

Her name is "Susan." She lives in West Paducah, Kentucky. Every time a new school shooting happens, she relives the terrifying nightmare of her own daughter's death on December 1, 1997. Her daughter was huddlcd with a group of students in a school hallway. They were holding hands and praying together when one of their classmates gunned them down. When Susan heard about the Littleton, Colorado, rampage, she couldn't stop crying. She kept saying, over and over through her tears, "It's December 1, 1997, all over again. When will we learn? How many more times does this have to happen?" ("Shooting Rampage, No Escape from Pain of Memories, Other Cities Reliving Littleton's Terror," *Houston Chronicle*, 21 April 1999, sec. A, p. 10.)

A teenager in Springfield, Oregon, survived a school assault there on May 21, 1998. She saw four students go down and twenty more injured. After that horrifying experience, she said, "Maybe we will learn this time. Maybe we will learn this time." But later, when she heard the news from Littleton, Colorado, she remarked, "We don't learn. We don't learn."

The point is clear: What we haven't learned, what we have *mis*learned, what we refuse to learn can *hurt* us! *does* hurt us! *will* hurt us!

There is a flippant little saying that we hear and use quite a lot. It goes like this: What you don't know won't hurt you. This saying has a partial truth in it. We can all think of certain, unique situations where that might fit. But by and large, *it is not true!* Ignorance is not a virtue. Ignorance is a terrible thing and, often, a very sinful thing.

What we don't know can hurt us terribly.

In the community where I grew up, in Memphis, Tennessee, we had an expression that was used mostly to tease people in good fun. The expression was this: "What you know would make a book. What you don't know would make a bigger book!" Over the years, I have thought of this expression many times, because I realize how very much we have yet to learn. Ignorance is not bliss. It is often the symbol of laziness and mixed-up priorities and blatant sinfulness.

In Luke 19, we see Jesus talking about this. He comes to Jerusalem and weeps over the moral blindness of the religious leaders of the day, and he says, "Would that even today you knew the things that make for peace! But now they are hid from your eyes" (verse 41 RSV). And in explaining the reason why the people stand apart from God, Jesus says, "Because you did not know the time of your visitation [from God]" (verse 44*b* RSV). Pay close attention to those first five words: *Because you did not know.* And just a few pages later in Luke's Gospel, Jesus speaks from the cross these gracious but haunting words: "Father, forgive them; for *they do not know* what they are doing" (23:34, emphasis added).

The message is obvious: What We Don't Know Will Hurt Us. Let me show you what I mean with three thoughts.

First of All, We Are Hurt Today by What We Have Not Yet Learned

There are so many things we do not know about life in this world, and what we don't know hurts us. We are doing things right now that will bring suffering to ourselves and to others, and yet we don't even realize it. Let me show you what I mean.

Go rent just about any movie that was made in the 1940s, and what you will notice is that most every character is smoking cigarettes. Most people didn't know back then that smoking could cause lung cancer and heart disease.

And just think of this. Just a little over a hundred years ago, we didn't know about germs. Before performing operations, surgeons would put on old, dirty overalls like an auto mechanic. Doctors didn't even bother to wash their hands before delivering a baby, and they had no idea that this practice had anything to do with so many babies and mothers dying in childbirth.

It makes you wonder, doesn't it? What will future generations say about us and the things we don't know or the things we unwittingly are doing that bring about our own suffering? Is it possible that people a hundred years from now will look back at our time and say: "Look what those people back there at the dawn of the millennium did! Why, of all things, they made assault weapons readily available and easily accessible to anyone who wanted them! Why, my goodness, they taught people how to make bombs on the Internet! Is it any wonder that they had so much violence back then? But, they just didn't know any better, bless their hearts!"

The truth is that "we are living in a time of taller buildings, but shorter tempers; wider freeways, but narrower viewpoints; higher incomes, but lower morals; more knowledge, but less wisdom; fancier houses, but broken homes. We have conquered outer space, but not inner space; learned to make a living, but not a life; added years to our life, but not life to our years. We spend too recklessly, drive too fast, laugh too little, anger too quickly, condemn too harshly, stay up too late, get up too tired, read too little, watch TV too much, and pray too seldom" (*Sunday Sermons* 29, no. 3 [May/June 1999]: 37). In short, we have more knowledge, but less wisdom. Now, of course, this is not true of all of us. But it *is* pretty descriptive of our present-day culture.

In Luke 19, we read of how Jesus wept over the moral blindness and spiritual ignorance of the people back then. I sometimes wonder if he looks down upon us today and weeps over the ways in which we hurt ourselves because of the things, first of all, that we have not yet learned.

Second, We Are Hurt Today by What We Have Mislearned

This is a darker ignorance to deal with. It is called prejudice. It is called bigotry. It is called racism. It is called ethnic cleansing.

There is a haunting and powerful line from the Broadway musical *South Pacific*. Painfully, the singer sings these words:

You've got to be taught to hate and fear,
You've got to be taught from year to year. . . .
("You've Got to Be Carefully Taught," lyrics by Oscar Hammerstein II)

As the song ironically points out, we do not come into this world filled with prejudice and bigotry and hatred. We learn those things from one another through racial slurs and ethnic jokes. Or better put, those are the things we *mis*learn.

If you will look at the beginning of Luke 19, you will see a beautiful thing. It's found in the Zacchaeus story recorded in the first ten verses of this chapter. The beautiful thing is this: Jesus called Zacchaeus by name. "Zacchaeus, jump down from that sycamore tree quickly! I want to have lunch with you." Jesus called him by his personal name. Everybody else in town had other names for Zacchaeus, and they weren't complimentary. People had assigned harsh, perhaps even profane names to Zacchaeus. To them, he wasn't a person—certainly not a brother. He was, in their minds, a thief, a traitor, a turncoat, a tax collector. They had labeled Zacchaeus. But Jesus called him by name.

I love that, because I know how dangerous, how destructive, and how painful prejudicial labels can be. When I was twelve years old, one of my school buddies slipped a pack of cigarettes out of the glove compartment of his dad's car. He promptly lit one up. Then he offered me a cigarette. And when I said "no thanks," he called me a "yellow-backed scaredy-cat." Now, that was a life-changing moment for me. From that moment on, I have *never* liked labels!

In his book *Living, Loving and Learning* ([Thorofare, N.J.: Charles B. Slack, 1982], p. 21), Leo Buscaglia puts it like this: "We ... create words and words are supposed to free us. Words are supposed to make us able to communicate. But words become boxes and bags in which we become trapped." *Labels.* We don't even know what they mean.

Hispanic; African American; Asian; liberal; conservative; redneck; Catholic; Protestant; Jew; ethnic Albanian; nerd; jock; geek; preppy; we hear the label, and we think we know everything about that person. But no one bothers to ask:

Does this person cry?
Does he feel?
Does she understand?
Does she have hopes and dreams?
Does he love his children?

Labels are so destructive. They teach fear and hatred and prejudice and bigotry, and they cause us to miss the integrity and uniqueness of the other person.

At the beginning of *The United Methodist Hymnal*, you can find John Wesley's "Directions for Singing." One of John Wesley's rules for singing is that if you have mis-learned a hymn, if you have learned to sing a hymn incorrectly, then you should "unlearn it as soon as you can." That's what I would say to you about our prejudice: Unlearn it as soon as you can.

In Luke 19, Jesus wept over the prejudice and bigotry of the people back then. He wept over the things they had mislearned. I sometimes wonder if he looks down upon us and weeps over the ways we hurt one another because of the hateful things we have mislearned.

We are hurt, first of all, by the things we haven't learned yet. And second, we are hurt by the things we have mislearned.

Third and Finally, We Are Hurt Today by the Things We Refuse to Learn

There is yet another kind of ignorance that haunts and hurts us. It is called the sin of the closed mind.

There is a "Peanuts" cartoon where Charlie Brown is running for his life. Lucy is chasing him with clenched fists. She shouts, "I'll catch you, Charlie Brown! I'll catch you, and when I do, I'm going to knock your block off!" Suddenly Charlie Brown screeches to a halt and says, "Wait a minute, Lucy. If you and I as relatively small children with relatively small problems can't sit down and talk through our problems, how can we expect the nations of the world to . . . " Pow! Lucy slugs him and says, "I had to hit him quick; he was beginning to make sense!"

Well, this is precisely what the closed-minded people of the first century did to Jesus. They hit him quick with a cross because he was beginning to make sense, and they didn't want to hear that. They didn't want their small, narrow, set, rigid "thought-world" disturbed.

They refused to listen. They refused to learn. All he said to them was, "Love God and love one another," but they refused to learn this. In fact, they were so infuriated by it that not only did they refuse to listen and learn, but worse, they tried to use violence to silence Jesus.

Some years ago, President George Bush Sr. called upon us to be "a kinder, gentler nation," but we didn't listen, did we? We haven't learned that lesson yet. Look at the entertainment world and its incessant depiction of graphic violence. I saw Tom Hanks talking about this on television one night, and he said, "It's not just the violence. It's violence with no consequences. The [characters played by the] movie star and his girlfriend blow somebody away and then drop off in a restaurant to have lunch. It's violence with no consequence. That's what is so bad about it."

And look at the news media today. What is their philosophy? "If it bleeds, it leads! Gotta get those ratings!" And sometimes they do their own brand of "bloodletting." Dan Rather once said that there are three kinds of reporters. There are lapdogs, watchdogs, and attack dogs. Rather said that reporters are supposed to be watchdogs, but more and more today, he said, we see them acting as attack dogs.

And look at us in our own cruel gossip sessions. When will we ever learn? Jesus told us a long time ago that our harsh, condemning judgments of others are wrong, and that our hateful criticisms will boomerang on us and come back to haunt us. But we refuse to learn this! We still think we can make ourselves look good by making others look bad, and we don't see that *we* are the ones who come off looking ugly in the process.

And look at the moral decline in our nation. Correspondent Jack Anderson spoke to the Washington Press Club recently, and said, "The greatest danger facing this nation or any nation is moral decay." Anderson was asked what we could do to reverse this moral decline, and he responded with three rules worth remembering:

If it isn't right, don't do it!
If it isn't true, don't say it!
If it isn't yours, don't take it!

Now, in the wake of the Littleton, Colorado, tragedy and others like it, let me say something to the children and young people of our world today. The world may confuse you about what is right and what is wrong, about what is good and bad, but here is something you can count on: Violence is wrong! Cruelty is wrong! Revenge is wrong! Hatred is wrong! If you will love God and love people—if you will make that the priority of your life—then everything else will fall in place for you!

Now, let me say a special word to parents: Stay close to your kids! Know who their friends are! Keep the lines of communication open with them! And tell them every day that you love them, and that they are special!

In recent times, as I have tried to grapple with the news of violence in our world, in our cities, in our schools, I have found myself recalling a true story. It happened some years ago up north. A little girl was lost in the woods. It was wintertime, snowing, sleeting, and bitterly cold. Hundreds of people combed the forest, desperately searching for the little girl. Time was of the essence. They knew she couldn't survive long in that freezing weather. For hours they looked, but had no luck. Finally, the searchers came up with the idea of joining hands so they could walk through the forest in a single line. They tried it, and in less than fifteen minutes they found the little girl! But it was too late. She had died from the cold and exposure. In the hush of that awful moment, someone said, "Why, oh why, didn't we join hands sooner?"

When I think about the troubles and conflicts in our world today, I think about that. "Why, oh why, can't we join hands? Why, oh why, can't we learn to come together in the love of Jesus Christ?" Please don't miss this. Don't miss the dramatic lessons of life.

❧ 15 ❧
Don't Miss . . .
God's Call to Come Home

Scripture: Psalm 42:1-6*a*

*H*ave you heard the story about the very boring, highly negative, extremely judgmental guest preacher who had been invited to preach at the Yale University Chapel? He took the word *Yale* as his outline, and he let each letter, *Y-A-L-E*, serve as a point of his sermon.

He said the *Y* stood for "youth," and he preached for twenty boring, wearisome, negative minutes on the failings of today's youth.

Then he said the letter *A* stood for "apathy," and he preached for twenty more judgmental, tiresome minutes about the apathy in our nation these days.

Next, he said the letter *L* stood for "laziness," and he droned on for another twenty minutes on how lazy people are in our time.

Finally, he came to the letter *E* in the word *Yale*. (He had already preached for over an hour at this point.) He said that the *E* stood for "emptiness," and he railed on for twenty more boring, negative, judgmental, tedious minutes on "emptiness."

Finally—*finally*—he was through. At the conclusion of the service, the choir and the guest preacher recessed down the center aisle. On the last row, the preacher saw a freshman student down on his knees, praying fervently. The guest preacher was thrilled to see that his message had so inspired this Yale student. The preacher stopped and asked the young man what he had said in his sermon that had so moved the freshman student to "such fervent prayer." The student answered, "I was just thanking God that I go to Yale, and not to the Massachusetts Institute of Technology; that would have taken eleven hours and twenty minutes!"

God forgive us when we make the exciting and thrilling message of the Christian gospel sound boring or negative or judgmental! God forgive us when we make the greatest news this world has ever heard seem tedious or dull or wearisome.

The word *gospel* literally means "good news," and the good news is that we can come home to God. No matter how far away we may have strayed or drifted or run, we can come home to God, and God will welcome us with open arms.

Let me ask you something. Do you ever feel uneasy or anxiety-ridden or cynical or surly? Do you ever feel out of sorts and out of sync? When we have those negative thoughts and feelings rumbling around in our souls, those are dramatic signs that we are "homesick for God." Let me show you what I mean.

Many years ago in England, a circus elephant named Bozo was very popular with the public. Children especially loved to crowd around his cage and throw him peanuts. But then one day, there was a sudden change in the elephant's personality. Bozo the elephant suddenly seemed angry and irritable and even hostile toward the children, and he tried to attack his keeper.

The decision was made: Bozo would have to be destroyed! The circus owner, a greedy and crude man, planned to stage a public execution of the animal. In this way, he could sell tickets and try to recoup some of the cost of losing such a valuable property. The day came, and the huge circus tent was packed. Bozo was in a large cage in the center ring. Nearby stood a firing squad with high-powered rifles. The manager was nearly ready to give the signal to fire, when out of the crowd came a short, inconspicuous man in a brown derby hat. "There is no need to do this," he told the manager quietly.

The manager brushed him aside. "He is a bad elephant. He must be destroyed before he hurts someone."

"You are wrong about that," insisted the man. "Just give me two minutes in the cage alone with him and I will prove you are wrong!"

The manager turned and stared in amazement. "You will be killed," he said.

"I don't think so," said the man. "Do I have your permission?"

The manager, being the kind of man he was, was not about to pass up a dramatic spectacle like this. Even if the man were killed, the publicity alone would be worth a fortune. "All right," he said, "but first you will have to sign a release absolving the circus of all responsibility." The small man in the brown derby hat signed the paper. As he next removed his coat and hat and prepared to enter Bozo's cage, the manager told the people what was about to happen.

A hush fell over the crowd. The door to the cage was unlocked, and the man stepped inside. When Bozo the elephant saw the stranger in his cage, he threw back his trunk, gave a mighty roar, then bent his head, ready to charge. The man stood perfectly still, a faint smile on his face as he began to talk to the animal. The audience was so quiet that those on the front rows could hear the man talking, but they couldn't make out the words. He seemed to be talking in some strange, foreign language.

Slowly, as the man continued to talk, the elephant

raised his head. Then the crowd heard an almost piteous cry from the elephant as his enormous head began to sway gently from side to side. Smiling now, the man walked confidently to the animal and began to stroke and pat its long trunk. All aggression seemed suddenly to have been drained from the elephant. Docile as a puppy now, Bozo wrapped his trunk around the man's waist, picked him up gently, and the two walked slowly around the ring. The crowd stood on their feet, cheering and applauding in amazement.

After a while the man said good-bye to the elephant and left the cage. "He's all right now," he told the manager. "You see, he's an Indian elephant, and none of you spoke his language, Hindustani. I would advise you to get someone around here who speaks it. You see, Bozo was just homesick."

With that, the man picked up his coat and hat and left. The astounded manager wondered who in the world the man was. Then he remembered the release slip the man had signed. He pulled it out and saw the name: Rudyard Kipling! (Adapted from Daniel T. Hannon, "Possibilities Unlimited," *Wings of Eagles* 5, no. 46 [November 25, 1997]: 1.)

Now, the point is clear. Like Bozo the elephant, when we get sullen and irritable and ill-tempered, when we feel grouchy and grumpy and fractious, when we get selfish and hostile and antagonistic, those are sure-fire signs of our being "homesick for God."

"Homesickness for God"; that's what the psalmist is talking about in the Forty-second Psalm:

> As a deer longs for flowing streams,
>   so my soul longs for you, O God.
> My soul thirsts for God,
>   for the living God. (verses 1-2*a*)

There is a spot in our hearts that only God can fill, and when we try to fill that emptiness with something other than God, then like Bozo the elephant, we get out of sorts and out of sync because we are "homesick for God." But the good news is that we can come home, and God will welcome us home with open arms.

Now, let me bring this closer to home with three thoughts.

First of All, We Can Come Home to God's Presence

We can live each day in the presence of God. Indeed, that's what we are supposed to do. That's the way God set it up. God intended for us to stay close to him, to live every moment in his presence.

Now, there are many things in our world that fascinate me beyond description. The miracle of the telephone is one of them. It boggles my mind to think that we can push a few buttons on our telephone and in a matter of seconds be talking to someone thousands of miles away.

I am also fascinated by television and computers and the Internet. I can type in a few words on my computer, push a button, and immediately get driving instructions to anywhere I want to go, complete with maps and a step-by-step guide of every turn in the journey. It is absolutely amazing what computers and the World Wide Web can do!

But as impressed as I am with the miraculous technology of our time, I am even more in awe of a phenomenon that happens year after year on the day of March 19. Do you have any idea what I'm talking about? For more than two hundred years, on March 19, the swallows have faithfully returned to the southern

California city of San Juan Capistrano, on exactly that day! They will do it again this year. March 19 is official- ly the last day of winter. Spring begins each year on March 20, whether there is snow on the ground and the temperatures are below freezing, or whether the skies are balmy and temperatures are in the high 80s. March 19 marks the end of winter, and March 20 begins the spring season. And somehow, miraculously, these little birds *know* that March 19 is the day for them to return to Capistrano. How do they *know* this? I mean, every four years there is a leap year, when instead of there being twenty-eight days in February, there are twenty-nine, but apparently this doesn't faze those little swallows at all. They somehow know how to compute that subtle differ- ence and to show up again on exactly March 19. It's phe- nomenal, really—one of the great mysteries and marvels of nature that no one understands. They just come home!

Recently, as I was thinking about this, I realized that deep down inside us, there is a homing instinct. There is something deep down inside of us that hungers and thirsts for home. Whether we realize it or not, we all yearn to come home to God. This is precisely what Psalm 42 is about, and this is what St. Augustine was talking about when he wrote what has become his most famous quote: "My soul is restless, O God, till it finds its rest in Thee."

The hymn writers of our faith realize this truth, and often they write of "coming home" to be with God. Remember the words from the famous gospel hymn: "Softly and tenderly Jesus is calling, / calling for you and for me... / Come home, come home; / you who are weary, come home" ("Softly and Tenderly Jesus Is Calling," Will L. Thompson, 1880).

That's number one. We can come home to God's presence.

Second, We Can Come Home
to God's Sacrificial Love

This is what John 3:16 is all about. Let me paraphrase it for us:

> For God so loved the world that he sacrificially gave his only Son, so that everyone who believes in him [whoever comes home to God through him] may not perish but may have eternal life.

Sacrificial love is the single most powerful thing in all the world. For example:

> February 15, 1921. New York City. The operating room of the Kane Summit Hospital. A doctor is performing an appendectomy.
>
> In many ways the events leading to the surgery are uneventful. The patient has complained of severe abdominal pain. The diagnosis is clear: an inflamed appendix. Dr. Evan O'Neill Kane is performing the surgery. In his distinguished thirty-seven-year medical career, he has performed nearly four thousand appendectomies, so this surgery will be uneventful in all ways except two.
>
> The first novelty of this operation? The use of local anesthesia in major surgery. Dr. Kane is a crusader against the hazards of general anesthesia. He contends that a local application is far safer. Many of his colleagues agree with him in principle, but in order for them to agree in practice, they will have to see the theory applied.
>
> Dr. Kane searches for a volunteer, a patient who is willing to undergo surgery while under local anesthesia. A volunteer is not easily found. Many are squeamish at the thought of being awake during their own surgery. Others are fearful that the anesthesia might wear off too soon.
>
> Eventually however, Dr. Kane finds a candidate. On Tuesday morning, February 15, the historic operation occurs.

The patient is prepped and wheeled into the operating room. A local anesthetic is applied. As he has done thousands of times, Dr. Kane dissects the superficial tissues and locates the appendix. He skillfully excises it and concludes the surgery. During the procedure, the patient complains of only mild discomfort.

The volunteer is taken into post-op, then placed in a hospital ward. He recovers quickly and is dismissed two days later.

Dr. Kane had proven his theory. Thanks to the willingness of a brave volunteer, Kane demonstrated that local anesthesia was a viable and even, in some cases, preferable alternative.

But as I said, there were two facts that made the surgery unique. I've told you the first: the use of local anesthesia. The second is the patient. The courageous candidate for surgery by Dr. Kane was Dr. Kane.

To prove his point, Dr. Kane operated on himself!

A wise move. The doctor became a patient in order to convince the patients to trust the doctor. (Max Lucado, *In the Eye of the Storm* [Dallas: Word Publishing, 1991], pp. 35-36)

There is nothing in the world more powerful than sacrificial love. If you ever wonder about that, just look at the cross and remember the power and wonder of God's sacrificial love for us through Jesus Christ. Jesus went to the cross in sacrificial love to bring us home to God.

We can come home to God's presence, and we can come home to God's sacrificial love.

Third and Finally, We Can
Come Home to God's Grace

In language we all can understand, *grace* means "getting the break you don't deserve, getting forgiveness you don't deserve."

The United Methodist General Commission on Communication has prepared a series of television spots about The United Methodist Church that is being shown nationwide. These television spots are designed to show people that they are wanted and welcome in The United Methodist Church. The message to viewers is that they can *come home* to the church, and they will be greeted with open arms. I have seen several of the spots. My favorite is called "Keys to the Kingdom," and it's about amazing grace.

The spot shows two junior-high-age boys climbing a fence at night. Then they pick a lock on a door and slip into a United Methodist church. They sneak through the sanctuary like two robbers, and then they go down to the basement to where the pool table is located. They turn on the lights and start playing pool, constantly looking over their shoulders, scared to death they are going to get caught. One of them takes a shot with the pool cue, and the ball jumps off the table, rolls across the floor, and stops when it hits a black shoe, which just happens to be on the foot of the pastor. There's a close-up of the boys' faces, and they look scared, terrified, and anxious. They have been caught. Across the screen come the words: *A true story.*

The boys are expecting the worst. *Big trouble.* But then the pastor says, "Of all the people in this neighborhood, you guys are trying the hardest to get into this church." Then the pastor reaches out and opens his hand. In it is a key to the church. He says to the boys, "Here, come any time you want!"

Next there is a close-up of the face of one of those boys. He takes a big breath, gives a sigh of relief, and then smiles. The frame freezes on that young boy, and across the screen come these words: *Now a Pastor.*

The spot concludes with these words: *The United*

Methodist Church: Offering hope and forgiveness. Offering Christ.

That's what it's all about, isn't it? Through Jesus Christ, we can be forgiven. We can come home to God's presence, to God's sacrificial love, and to God's grace.

Whatever you do in this life, don't miss that. Please don't miss the homecoming party that God has planned for you!

Study Guide

Written by John D. Schroeder

This book by James W. Moore offers insights on how not to miss the gifts of God when God comes near. As a leader, you have the opportunity to help the members of your group become more effective Christians. Here are some suggestions to keep in mind as you begin:

1. You should review the entire book before your first group meeting so that you have an overview of the book and can be a better guide for the members of your group. You may want to use a highlighter to designate important points in the text.

2. Give a copy of the book to each participant before the first session and ask participants to read the introduction before your initial meeting. You may wish to limit the size of your group to ensure that everyone gets a chance to participate. Not everyone may feel comfortable reading aloud, answering questions, or participating in group discussion or activities. Let group members know that this is okay, and encourage them to participate as they feel comfortable in doing so.

3. Begin each session by reviewing the main points using the chapter summary. You may ask group members what they saw as highlights. Use your own reading, any notes you have taken, and this study guide to suggest other main points.

4. Select the discussion questions and activities you plan to use in advance. Use those you think will work best with your group. You may want to ask the questions in a different order from the way they are presented in the study guide. Allow a reasonable amount of time for questions and a reasonable amount of time for one or two activities. You may create your own questions and activities if you desire.

5. Before moving from questions to activities, ask members if they have any questions that have not been answered.

6. Following the conclusion of the final activity, close with a short prayer. If your group desires, pause for individual prayer requests.

7. Start your meetings on time and end them on schedule.

8. If you ask a question and no one volunteers an answer, begin the discussion by suggesting an answer yourself. Then ask for comments and other answers.

9. Encourage total participation by asking questions of specific members. Your role is to give everyone who desires it the opportunity to talk and to be involved. Remember, you can always ask such questions as "Why?" and "Can you explain in more detail?" to continue and deepen a discussion.

10. Be thankful and supportive. Thank members for their ideas and participation.

Introduction: God Was Here, and I Was Out to Lunch

Chapter Summary

1. God comes near us, but we often don't sense his presence.

2. Sometimes, blinded by the law, we miss the chance to love.

3. Sometimes, blinded by common practice, we miss the common sense.
4. Sometimes, blinded by our systems, we miss the Savior.

Reflection / Discussion Questions

1. What new insights did you receive from reading this chapter?
2. What causes us to be "blinded" by the old, so that we miss the new?
3. Why do you think people are threatened by or uncomfortable with new things?
4. According to the author, why was Jesus a "marked man" in Mark 3?
5. What caused the Pharisees to be jealous of Jesus?
6. How important was ritual to the Pharisees? How important was it to Jesus?
7. Share an example from your life or from the life of someone you know on being blinded by the law.
8. When blinded by the law, what do we miss?
9. Give an example of when love or understanding must supersede law.
10. Recall a time when you were blinded by common practice and missed common sense.
11. What causes us to do things our own way instead of God's way?
12. Recall a time you missed an opportunity because you were "out to lunch."

Practical Applications / Activities

1. As individual group members, talk about why you decided to read this book and /or what you hope to gain from reading it.

2. Examine a newspaper or a magazine for examples of new ways that threaten people or make them uncomfortable.
3. On your own, use a Bible commentary or another resource to to learn more about the Pharisees and their rituals.
4. Try something that is new and uncomfortable for you this week. Report your results to the group next week.

Prayer: *Dear God, you come near us, yet we are often distant and unaware of your love and presence. Help us to not be blinded to opportunities to serve you and others. Thank you for your gifts that help us tackle any situation. Be with us this week. Amen.*

Chapter 1: Don't Miss...The Call to Discipleship

Chapter Summary

1. There is more to life than just sitting there doing the same old things.
2. We miss the call to discipleship if we just sit there in defeat.
3. We miss the call to discipleship if we just sit there in apathy.
4. We miss the call to discipleship if we just sit there in indecision.

Reflection / Discussion Questions

1. What new insights did you receive from reading this chapter?
2. Share a time when you felt you were trapped in a routine and in a rut.

3. What do you think causes people to get trapped in routines?
4. Discuss the difference between being *able* and being *available.*
5. Which story in this chapter made an impact on you? Explain.
6. In your own words, explain what it means to "sit there in defeat."
7. What does Jesus say to us about overcoming defeat?
8. Talk about a time when you tried to overcome defeat.
9. In your own words, explain the meaning of *apathy.*
10. What is the difference between apathy and defeat?
11. What do you think causes indecision? What holds us back?
12. Recall a time of indecision in your life.

Practical Applications / Activities

1. Discuss the two kinds of desires working within us.
2. As a group, talk about times when you wanted to "just sit there," but moved forward anyway.
3. As a group, share your ideas on discipleship. How do we begin? What are the qualifications?
4. Discuss what duties God expects of us as disciples. As a group, write a job description for being a disciple.
5. Examine and weigh the costs and benefits of being a disciple.

Prayer: *Dear God, forgive us when we go our own ways and miss your call to be your disciple. Help us to be your heart, hands, and feet on this earth and to serve you. Thank you for giving us all we need to be disciples. May we follow your ways and your call this week. Amen.*

Chapter 2: Don't Miss...The Spirit of Christ

Chapter Summary

1. We want the Spirit of Christ to be alive, but someone else to do the work.
2. People need to see Christ's spirit of forgiveness in you.
3. People need to see Christ's spirit of love in you.
4. People need to see Christ's spirit of ministry in you.

Reflection / Discussion Questions

1. What new insights did you receive from reading this chapter?
2. Which story in this chapter made an impact on you? Explain.
3. What causes us to miss the Spirit of Christ?
4. What does it mean to be a reflector of Christ's light?
5. Talk about someone you know who reflects the light of Christ.
6. In your own words, what does it mean to forgive and to be forgiven?
7. Recall a time when you were forgiven by someone. How did you feel?
8. What makes it difficult to forgive someone?
9. What does it mean to love one another as Christ has loved you?
10. What prevents us from loving one another? What enables us to love one another?
11. Discuss the qualifications for being active in ministry.
12. Why do we want someone else to "be Jesus" for the world?

Practical Applications / Activities

1. As a group, list some ways we can be reflectors of Christ's light.
2. List some ways we can live in a spirit of reconciliation and forgiveness.
3. As a group, weigh the costs and the benefits of forgiving someone.
4. Discuss this statement: "The greatest satisfaction is in service."

Prayer: *Dear God, we want to reflect the light of Christ, but often we fall short. Forgive us and help us love, forgive, and minister to others as you would do. Be with us as we begin a new week of ministry to others. Amen.*

Chapter 3: Don't Miss ... Having Your Eyes *"Christ-ed"*

Chapter Summary

1. We please God when we act.
2. Having your eyes *Christ*-ed changes the way you see yourself.
3. Having your eyes *Christ*-ed changes the way you see others.
4. Having your eyes *Christ*-ed changes the way you see God.

Reflection / Discussion Questions

1. What new insights did you receive from reading this chapter?
2. Share an "eye-opening" experience from your youth that gave you new insight.

3. What lessons do we learn in John 9 from Jesus' healing the man who was blind?
4. In your own words, explain what it means to have your eyes "*Christ*-ed."
5. How did the Pharisees react to Jesus' healing the man who was blind? What were the reasons for their reaction?
6. How did the disciples react to seeing the man who was blind?
7. Which story in this chapter made an impact on you?
8. Why is the word *anointed* important in John 9:6?
9. Recall a time that you were blinded by selfishness. What was the result?
10. According to the author, when we "see with our hearts," what happens?
11. How has your perception of God changed over time?
12. What happens to us when we spend more time with Jesus?

Practical Applications / Activities

1. As a group, look at John 9 from four viewpoints: that of the man who was blind, that of Jesus, that of the disciples, and that of the Pharisees. Putting yourself in the place of each person or group, discuss the events in this passage of Scripture, as well as possible consequences.
2. Discuss this statement: "True sight is always a matter of the heart, not the eyes."
3. Make an effort to see people differently during the coming week.
4. Do a self-examination this week regarding how you see yourself.

Prayer: *Dear God, open our eyes so that we may see you and see those in need. Forgive our blindness to the* problems of others. Help us see clearly what you want us to do, and then help us take action. Thank you for keeping your eyes always on us. Amen.

Chapter 4: Don't Miss...The Gift of Amazing Grace

Chapter Summary

1. Christian love takes the initiative.
2. Jesus shows us how to love.
3. Jesus wants us to break down the barriers that divide.
4. Change comes from unconditional love.

Reflection / Discussion Questions

1. What new insights did you receive from reading this chapter?
2. Which story in this chapter made an impact on you?
3. In your own words, explain the meaning of "amazing grace."
4. Why is amazing grace called a gift? What do we have to do to receive it?
5. What causes people to miss the gift of amazing grace?
6. How did Jesus' encounter with the woman at the well demonstrate amazing grace?
7. What are some of the barriers that divide us from others?
8. Recall a time when you took the initiative or someone took the initiative to help you.
9. In your own words, explain the meaning of unconditional love.
10. Who has shown you unconditional love? Explain.
11. What causes us to love someone unconditionally?

12. How has reading this chapter helped you?

Practical Applications / Activities

1. Contrast the life of the woman at the well before and after meeting Jesus.
2. Share with someone this week what you learned from this lesson.
3. As a group, list some ways that Christians can break down barriers.
4. Show unconditional love to someone this week.

Prayer: *Dear God, thank you for your amazing grace. Help us share your love with others and break down the barriers that divide us. May we love others as you love us. Be with us this week and always. Amen.*

Chapter 5: Don't Miss ... The Power of the Cross

Chapter Summary

1. The cross is the central focus of our Christian faith.
2. The cross reminds us of the ugliness of sin.
3. The cross reminds us of the beauty of sacrifice.
4. The cross reminds us of the power of salvation.

Reflection / Discussion Questions

1. What new insights did you receive from reading this chapter?
2. Which story in this chapter made an impact on you?
3. When did you first realize the power of the cross?
4. In your own words, explain what the power of the cross means to you.

5. What does the cross remind us about sin?
6. What does the cross remind us about the beauty of sacrifice?
7. What does the cross remind us about God's love for us?
8. Recall a time when someone made a sacrifice for you.
9. Recall a time when you sacrificed for someone else. Why did you make the sacrifice, and how did it make you feel?
10. What does the cross remind us about the power of salvation?
11. How does the cross challenge us?
12. How has your faith and your view of the cross been shaped or strengthened as a result of your study of this chapter?

Practical Applications / Activities

1. Discuss whether or not we sometimes take the cross for granted because we see it so much. Has its widespread use in society diluted its meaning?
2. Meditate on the power of the cross this week.
3. As a group, read an account of the crucifixion of Jesus in the Bible.
4. Share with someone this week something you learned from this chapter.

Prayer: *Dear God, the cross reminds us of so many things. It reminds us of your love, your power, your sacrifice, and the ugliness of sin. Help us not to take your cross for granted, but to make it the focus of our faith. Thank you for your love and for being here with us during our time together. Amen.*

Chapter 6: Don't Miss...The Great Promises of Easter

Chapter Summary

1. God promises to always be with us.
2. Easter gives us the gift of a resurrection.
3. Easter gives us the gift of a mission.
4. Easter gives us the gift of a promise.

Reflection / Discussion Questions

1. What new insights did you receive from reading this chapter?
2. Which story in this chapter made an impact on you?
3. Share from your childhood a family Easter tradition.
4. Share an event or situation that made one Easter special for you.
5. What are some of the Easter traditions of your church?
6. According to the author, what does the Scripture outline as the special gifts of Easter?
7. Recall a time when someone shared his or her faith with you, and how it made you feel.
8. In your own words, what does *mission* mean to you?
9. How important are promises to you? Explain.
10. Share a promise that someone made to you.
11. Who first shared with you the Easter story and the promises of Easter?
12. How did reading this chapter help make the Easter story more meaningful for you?

Practical Applications / Activities

1. Talk about ways to share your faith with others and how to tell the Easter story.

170

2. Use the Bible to locate the many promises of God.
3. Meditate on the great promises of Easter.
4. Share the message of this lesson with someone this week.

Prayer: *Dear God, thank you for the many promises of Easter. Thank you for the gift of resurrection, mission, and promise. Help us share the message of Easter with others and proclaim your love. May our faith continue to grow as we grow closer to you. Amen.*

Chapter 7: Don't Miss . . . The Rest of the Story

Chapter Summary

1. The Easter story does not end with the Resurrection.
2. Jesus wants to give us his love.
3. Jesus wants to give us his forgiveness.
4. Jesus wants to give us his ministry.

Reflection / Discussion Questions

1. What new insights did you receive from reading this chapter?
2. Which story in this chapter had an impact on you?
3. Recall something that happened to you or your family that had an unexpected ending.
4. What were the disciples expecting after the resurrection of Jesus?
5. What issues were the disciples dealing with after the Resurrection?
6. What three things did the risen Christ want to give to Simon Peter?
7. What is the first thing and the last thing that Jesus said to Simon Peter?

8. Share a time when you were forgiven and received a new beginning.
9. How did Simon Peter feel before and after talking to the risen Lord?
10. What was the specific reason for Jesus' breakfast meeting with the disciples?
11. In your own words, explain what ministry means to you.
12. How has reading this chapter helped you?

Practical Applications / Activities

1. Discuss how love makes you see people differently.
2. Discuss the breakfast-by-the-sea passage in John 21.
3. As a group, talk about how ministry is different from a job.
4. Share with someone this week what you learned from this lesson.

Prayer: *Dear God, thank you for going beyond the Resurrection and sharing with us the rest of the story. Thank you for your love, for your forgiveness, and for giving us your ministry. Help us love and forgive others as you love and forgive us. May we grow in love toward you and toward one another. Amen.*

Chapter 8: Don't Miss ... God's Surprises

Chapter Summary

1. All through the Scriptures, we see God surprising people.
2. Pentecost showed God's surprising love for all people.
3. Pentecost showed God's surprising presence in unexpected places.

172

4. Pentecost showed God's surprising judgment of what we fail to do.

Reflection / Discussion Questions

1. What new insights did you receive from reading this chapter?
2. Which story in this chapter had an impact on you?
3. Recall a time when you were surprised by someone or by an event.
4. Recall a time when you surprised someone. What was the person's reaction? How did you feel? Why did you surprise this person?
5. How were people surprised at Pentecost?
6. Besides the events of Pentecost, what are some of God's other surprises that are mentioned in this chapter?
7. Name some incidents where God was present in unexpected places.
8. Recall a time when God found you in an unexpected place.
9. In your own words, explain what "the sin of omission" means to you.
10. Name some people in the Bible who were guilty of the sin of omission.
11. Is there forgiveness for the sin of omission? Explain.
12. How has reading this chapter helped you?

Practical Applications / Discussion

1. Use the Bible to locate as many of God's surprises as you can find.
2. Surprise someone this week with love, forgiveness, or an unexpected act of kindness.
3. Reflect on or discuss how God has surprised you throughout your life.

4. This week, share with someone something you have learned from your reading or study of this chapter.

Prayer: *Dear God, thank you for always surprising us with signs of your presence and gracious love. Help us grow and mature in the faith as a result, and empower us to share your love with others. Be with us this week and always. Amen.*

Chapter 9: Don't Miss...The Chance for a Second Birth

Chapter Summary

1. When we accept Christ and commit our lives to him, we are born again.
2. We need to come alive to the Bible.
3. We need to come alive to love.
4. We need to come alive to eternal life.

Reflection / Discussion Questions

1. What new insights did you receive from reading this chapter?
2. What story in this chapter had an impact on you?
3. In your own words, explain what it means to be "born again" or to be "born from above."
4. Explain what it means to "come alive" to the Bible.
5. According to the author, what do we need in order to have the Bible come alive for us?
6. Describe your relationship or experience with the Bible. If possible, recall the first time the Bible came alive for you.
7. In this chapter, what Scripture verse does the author note as being "one of the greatest statements in all of the Bible," and why?

8. Why can't we earn the gift of being "born from above"?
9. Explain what it means to come alive to love.
10. What do Christians need to do in order to come alive to eternal life?
11. What person has helped you come alive in the Christian faith, and how?
12. How has reading this chapter helped you?

Practical Applications / Activities

1. We live in a world today much like that of Nicodemus. How do rules and regulations today prevent us from loving and helping others?
2. Discuss how the Pharisees saw Jesus compared to how Nicodemus saw him.
3. Meditate on the possibilities of second birth this week.
4. Share this lesson and the opportunity to come alive with someone this week.

Prayer: *Dear God, help us come alive to others, to the Bible, and to eternal life. Thank you for showing us the way through your Son, Christ Jesus. May we overcome all things that prevent us from reaching out to others, and be reflections of your love. Amen.*

Chapter 10: Don't Miss ... The Leap of Faith

Chapter Summary

1. It is dangerous to have a closed mind.
2. Pride prevents us from taking a leap of faith.
3. Procrastination prevents us from taking a leap of faith.

4. Fear prevents us from taking a leap of faith.

Reflection / Discussion Questions

1. What new insights did you receive from reading this chapter?
2. What story in this chapter had an impact on you?
3. Recall a time when you took a leap of faith.
4. Recall a time when you failed to take a leap of faith and missed an opportunity. What caused you to hesitate? How did you feel about the situation later?
5. What are the costs of taking a leap of faith?
6. Why didn't Naaman want to wash in the Jordan River? What made him do it?
7. In what ways do people today look for healing in the wrong places, and what is the cause of this?
8. Recall a time when you swallowed your pride. What happened as a result?
9. In your own words, explain what pride means to you.
10. Recall a time when you procrastinated, and share the result.
11. Which is more likely to stop you—fear, procrastination, or pride? Why?
12. How has reading this chapter helped you?

Practical Applications / Activities

1. Discuss strategies on how to get past roadblocks of pride.
2. Discuss strategies on how to get past roadblocks of fear.
3. Discuss strategies on how to get past roadblocks of procrastination.
4. Take a leap of faith this week. Report your results back to the group.

Prayer: *Dear God, there are so many roadblocks that we face each day in reaching out to you and to others. Help us take a leap of faith and know that you will be with us when we journey into the unknown. Thank you for always being there for us, and help us remember that you are only a prayer away. Amen.*

Chapter 11: Don't Miss . . . The Priorities of Life

Chapter Summary

1. Put the real priorities first.
2. Make commitment to Christ a top priority.
3. Make commitment to family a top priority.
4. Make commitment to the church a top priority.

Reflection / Discussion Questions

1. What new insights did you receive from reading this chapter?
2. What story in this chapter had an impact on you?
3. Who taught you about priorities, and how?
4. How have your priorities changed as you have grown older?
5. What are common priorities for individuals in high school? In college?
6. In your own words, explain what it means to make something a priority.
7. How can you determine whether you need to make a change in your priorities?
8. What does it mean to make Christ a priority?
9. What does it mean to make family a priority?
10. What does it mean to make the church a priority?
11. What are the costs and benefits of making priorities?
12. How has reading this chapter helped you?

Practical Applications / Activities

1. Discuss how you know whether a priority is right or wrong.
2. Discuss priorities for Christians and those for non-Christians.
3. Talk to people this week about priorities. Ask about their priorities. Share your priorities.
4. Make a list of your own priorities this week, and examine them individually and together. Ask yourself whether any changes are in order, and if so, create an action plan for making those changes.

Prayer: *Dear God, thank you for helping us learn more about priorities. Grant us wisdom to know what is important and what is not. Help us make you and your kingdom our priority, along with our family and the church family. Be with us this week. Amen.*

Chapter 12: Don't Miss... The Joy of Service

Chapter Summary

1. Each one of us has been given an instrument to play in Christ's church.
2. Decide where you are going to serve God.
3. Decide how you can best broadcast the gospel.
4. Each of us has within us a well of living water.

Reflection / Discussion Questions

1. What new insights did you receive from reading this chapter?
2. What story in this chapter had an impact on you?
3. What is your "instrument" in Christ's church? Explain.

4. When did you first become aware of your special gift from God?
5. The author describes three conversations that were important in shaping his direction and outlook. Briefly share a conversation that had an impact on you.
6. In your own words, explain what "the joy of service" means to you.
7. What people or events have shaped your decisions on serving God?
8. The author says that his decision to serve the local church is "a big part" of who he is. What decision or decisions have you made that determine "a big part" of who *you* are? Explain.
9. Drawing from your reading of this chapter, explain the difference between *broad*casting and *narrow*casting.
10. In your own words, explain this statement: "Every one of us has within us a well of living water."
11. Explain the meaning or significance of the author's "conversation number three."
12. How did reading this chapter help you?

Practical Applications / Activities

1. Discuss ways in which people can broadcast the gospel.
2. Discuss how we learn, grow, and benefit from service to others.
3. Meditate on or do a personal inventory of your unique talents—your special gifts from God.
4. Share with someone this week what you learned from this lesson.

Prayer: *Dear God, you give us joy. There is joy in serv-*
ing you and in serving others. Thank you for giving each

of us special gifts in order that we may use them in your service. Help us reach out to you and to others. Be with us during this coming week. Amen.

Chapter 13: Don't Miss ... The Spirit of Compassion

Chapter Summary

1. The best way to love God is to love God's children.
2. We are to perform our job as if we are working for God.
3. We are to speak words of love and encouragement to others.
4. We are to treat others as we would Christ.

Reflection / Discussion Questions

1. What new insights did you receive from reading this chapter?
2. What story in this chapter had an impact on you?
3. In your own words, explain what it means to have a spirit of compassion.
4. If we have compassion, how should we perform our job? Give examples.
5. If we have compassion, how should we speak to others?
6. If we have compassion, how should we treat others?
7. Recall a time when someone treated you with compassion. How did you feel?
8. Recall a time when you treated someone with compassion. What was the effect of this?
9. How would your work environment change if everyone brought a spirit of love and compassion to work?

10. In which area (job, words, deeds) do you need the most improvement? Why?
11. What often prevents us from having a spirit of compassion toward others? How can we overcome obstacles to our having and showing compassion?
12. How did reading this chapter help you?

Practical Applications / Activities

1. Examine the costs and benefits of living with a spirit of compassion.
2. Discuss how one person can make a difference by the way he or she speaks.
3. Reflect on your behavior toward others this week.
4. Reread passages in this chapter, and in ways of your choosing, take action this week to live in a spirit of compassion.

Prayer: *Dear God, grant us a spirit of compassion. May our thoughts, words, and deeds reflect love for others. Help us be patient, kind, helpful, and considerate each and every day. Thank you for having compassion for us. Amen.*

Chapter 14: Don't Miss ... The Dramatic Lessons of Life

Chapter Summary

1. Ignorance is a terrible thing, and often a very sinful thing.
2. We are hurt by what we have not yet learned.
3. We are hurt by what we have mislearned.
4. We are hurt by the things we refuse to learn.

Reflection / Discussion Questions

1. What new insights did you receive from reading this chapter?
2. What story in this chapter had an impact on you?
3. Recall an incident from your childhood regarding how you were affected by your own ignorance.
4. What causes us to feel wise when in reality we are not wise?
5. Explain the connection between ignorance and sinfulness.
6. Give an example of how we are hurt by what we have not learned.
7. Give an example of how we are hurt by what we have mislearned.
8. Give an example of how we are hurt by what we refuse to learn.
9. Discuss this statement: "We have more knowledge, but less wisdom."
10. Why do we label people? Have you ever been labeled? If so, how?
11. What does it actually take to learn from the dramatic lessons of life?
12. How has reading this chapter helped you?

Practical Applications / Activities

1. List some of the costs of ignorance.
2. Discuss labels and how we tend to mislearn.
3. Talk about some of the dramatic lessons you have experienced and how they have changed you.
4. Share what you have learned from this lesson with a family member or friend.

Prayer: *Dear God, you created life to be full of lessons for us. Life is a school of learning. We thank you for life and for all its ups and downs, while remembering that you are always with us. Grant us wisdom to avoid making mistakes and to learn from the mistakes that we do make. Please be with us all during the coming week. Amen.*

Chapter 15: Don't Miss... God's Call to Come Home

Chapter Summary

1. Our ills are because we are homesick for God.
2. We can come home to God's presence.
3. We can come home to God's sacrificial love.
4. We can come home to God's grace.

Reflection / Discussion Questions

1. What new insights did you receive from reading this chapter?
2. What story in this chapter had an impact on you?
3. Talk about a time when you were homesick.
4. What causes us to be homesick for God?
5. In your own words, what does it mean to come home to God's presence?
6. In your own words, what does it mean to come home to God's sacrificial love?
7. In your own words, what does it mean to come home to God's grace?
8. Share a story of sacrificial love from your life or from the life of someone you know.
9. Share a story of grace from your life or from the life of someone you know.
10. What are some signs and symptoms that we are homesick for God?

11. Name some cures for being homesick for God.
12. How were you helped by reading this chapter?

Practical Applications / Activities

1. Share how reading and studying this book has helped you.
2. Which chapter made the biggest impact on you, and why?
3. Discuss ways we can come home to God's presence.
4. Reflect this week on God's presence, love, and grace.

Prayer: *Dear God, we are often homesick for you. Help us remember that we can always come home to your presence, your love, and your grace. You are always with us. Keep us all in your care, this week and for always. Amen.*